A Proven 5-Step Plan To Unlock Your Superpowers To Create Impact, Connections, And Fulfillment

The GIVER Method

How To Transform Lives Through Generosity

Jake Talbert

Founder & Chief GIVER at The GIVER Method

✿ LUCKY BOOK PUBLISHING

To request permissions, contact the publisher at hello@luckybookpublishing.com.

Paperback ISBN: 978-1-998287-44-4
Hardcover ISBN: 978-1-998287-45-1
E-book ISBN: 978-1-998287-46-8

1st edition, November 2024

"As human beings, our job in life is to help people realize how rare and valuable each one of us really is, that each of us has something that no one else has or ever will have something inside that is unique to all time. It's our job to encourage each other to discover that uniqueness and to provide ways of developing its expression."

Mr. Rogers

My Gift To You

I am so glad you're here!

As my Gift to you, get FREE Access to the Audiobook
of The GIVER Method and other Free Book Bonuses by
scanning the QR Code below or visiting
TheGiverMethodBook.com

Contents

My Dream

Over the next 2 years, my dream is to help one million people discover their gifts and superpowers, guiding them to create meaningful change in their lives and communities through selfless giving. Would you like to be part of this journey?

Join our IMPACT Makers community and explore how coaching can help you unlock your full potential as a GIVER.

Please reach out if you would like me to speak to your audience about:

- Growing Through Giving: Discovering Your Hidden Superpowers

- From Self-Doubt to Self-Actualization: The GIVER Journey

- Overcoming 'Imposter Syndrome' By Becoming A True GIVER

- Building Deeper Connections Through Selfless Service

- Creating Value That Changes Lives

- Making Your Impact Both Intentional and Meaningful

- Transforming Communities One Gift at a Time
- Inviting the Universe to Pay You Back Through Giving

TheGiverMethod.com

Chapter 1:
The GIVER Method - Introduction

"What lies behind us and what lies before us are tiny matters compared to what lies within us." - Ralph Waldo Emerson

---

The Sea Of Cubicles

I remember the moment with startling clarity. There I was, hunched over my desk in the cramped confines of my cubicle, surrounded by the soulless hum of office life. It was an ordinary day in the corporate maze, a sea of cubicles stretching as far as the eye could see. Amidst the mundane, a conversation between co-workers caught my attention. It was a simple exchange, yet in that moment, it was as if I truly saw my world for the first time.

I realized I was just another face in the crowd, a cog in the vast machine of a large enterprise. While listening to their stories, it hit me: "I don't belong here." It wasn't just the physical space of the cubicle that confined me; it was the life I had unwittingly constructed around it—a life that felt increasingly alien and suffocating. I saw the toll it was taking on me, how it dulled my presence in the world, strained the relationships that mattered most, and left me feeling like a shadow of the husband, father, brother, son, and friend I aspired to be.

In that moment of stark revelation, I understood that my unique gifts, the very essence of who I was, were withering away in the neglect of the unremarkable and the routine. It was then that I made a vow to myself—a commitment not only to rediscover those gifts but to cultivate them into true superpowers. I would no longer be a passive participant in my own life; I would become a GIVER, dedicated to making a meaningful impact in the lives of my family, friends, co-workers, and everyone I encountered. This was the beginning of a journey that would reshape not just my own existence but ripple out to touch the lives of others in profound and lasting ways.

Hey there, I'm Jake, and my journey from a struggling employee to a thriving business leader, entrepreneur, and influencer is the living, breathing proof of everything you're about to explore. In this dizzyingly fast-paced world, where everyone's racing to make their mark, it often feels like we're just voices in a storm—shouting to be heard, yearning to make a real impact, but ending up feeling lost in an endless buzz. It's a world where connections can feel as fleeting as they are numerous, leaving us craving something deeper, something more meaningful. And here's the kicker: amidst this hustle, many of us are sitting on a treasure trove of untapped potential. I'm talking about those superpowers of ours—yes, superpowers—that we've either forgotten, never recognized, or simply underestimated.

Think about it for a moment. How often have we downplayed our unique talents or ignored our strengths because they didn't seem to fit into the conventional boxes society loves so much? Or maybe we've been too caught up in the daily grind to even notice them. It's like we're trying to build skyscrapers with our bare hands while leaving the most powerful tools locked away in the toolbox. These superpowers, our innate gifts, are like secret weapons that, when unleashed, can completely transform how we connect, influence, and create something truly valuable— not just in our businesses, but in our personal lives as well. It's time to craft a legacy that's uniquely ours, tapping into the magic that's been within us all along.

Enter The GIVER Method

Let me be clear: *The GIVER Method* isn't your run-of-the-mill self-help or personal development book. It's a life-changing way to approach how we live. It's about stepping into who you truly are, recognizing the untapped gifts and superpowers that live inside you, and learning how to harness those strengths not just for personal and business success, but for the greater good. It's about realizing that giving—when done with intention and authenticity—opens doors you never knew existed. Giving isn't just an exchange; it's a way to unlock your highest potential, and it rewards you in ways you never imagined.

The acronym GIVER itself captures the essence of this journey:

- G: Gift Giver – The unique strengths you have to offer to the world.

- I: Impactful Influence – The lasting effect of your actions and the legacy you build.

- V: Vivid Value – The clear and lasting difference you make by offering your best without expecting anything in return.

- E: Eager Engagement – The energy and passion you bring to each relationship.

- R: Relationship Riches – The deep, meaningful connections you build by giving freely.

Through the GIVER Method, you're going to discover/ re-discover your superpowers, unique gifts, and genius. I'm not talking about the everyday kind of skills like making a great cup of coffee or being able to multitask like a champ. I'm referring to those unique talents and strengths that are distinctly yours, eagerly waiting to be released upon the world. I firmly believe that every person harbors at least five gifts or superpowers that they should be able to identify and utilize in any scenario. By identifying and deploying your superpower, you're stepping into a world of engagement, influence, and fulfillment that you might have previously thought was reserved for a select few.

This method is a comprehensive guide with a toolkit for transformation and change in your life. It's about unlocking the true value in every smile, conversation, and interaction you have. Prepare to witness a shift in how you live your life. You'll begin to engage more authentically, influence more powerfully, and create value that's not only recognized but deeply appreciated. One of my gifts, or superpowers, is my ability to take people's complex problems and simplify them into an easier solution. This is a skill I use daily in my work, and it's what businesses pay good money for me and my team to help with.

I found myself being part of an amazing community called Archangel. In this community, everyone is so open, sincere, and giving. I identified myself as a GIVER and wanted to contribute in the best way I could. I started offering my gift to the members of this community, showing up to all the calls and events, sharing as much knowledge as I could, and helping many of them gain clarity in their businesses. Technically, the members of this community all qualified as ideal clients, but that was not my focus. My focus was on giving without expecting anything in return. Over time, I have grown very close to many of these community members. By implementing what The GIVER

Method teaches, I have seen the ways the universe has paid me back.

I never asked whether someone I was helping wanted to work with us. I just gave value, and as I did, the members of that community consistently asked me how they could work with us. Over time, this has become one of our biggest pools of clients, and it all started with being a GIVER.

What Does Being A GIVER Look Like?

Let's take a glimpse into the lives of those who've walked this path. Below are heartfelt reflections from GIVERs I've had the privilege to interview, sharing in their own words the transformative impact of living by these principles:

"I developed my superpowers. One of them is that I can see things for people they can't see for themselves. I can see possibilities. I can see potential that they may not be able to see for themselves. Now I help them change their lives forever by tapping into the possibilities that await them"

"Once I found the power of giving and expecting nothing in return I stepped out of my corporate job, started my company, put my stuff in storage, and started traveling. Ended up meeting my partner. And now we're married and we live on an island. - I just said yes to giving myself permission to do my life differently and just go for it."

"I feel a deeper connection with all those I come in contact with."

"I am more excited than ever to engage with my spouse and children. We are having deeper conversations and creating lasting memories that I know I was missing out on before."

"I found the more generous I am in giving the more blessings I seem to receive out of nowhere."

"I used to be protective of what I thought made me and my business special and we struggled, once I dropped the ego and shared my genius with others I found my business started taking off in ways I never thought possible."

These testimonials offer a window into the many ways 'The GIVER Method' can enrich your life, from deepening relationships to unlocking personal and professional growth. Each story is a testament to the power of giving and the profound changes it can bring about.

Exercises and Actionable Content

Becoming a GIVER requires more than just reading this book—it requires taking action. Each chapter includes exercises, action items, and worksheets to help you apply the principles discussed. It is highly recommended that you read the entire chapter before starting the exercises, action items, and worksheets.

You can access the Chapter 1 worksheet by going to www.thegivermethod.com/chapter-1-worksheets

---

Chapter 2: Gifted

Discovering Your Unique Gifts and Superpowers

"Everybody is a genius. But if you judge a fish by its ability to climb a tree, it will live its whole life believing that it is stupid." - Albert Einstein

---

The Power of Self-Discovery

When I set out to write this book, I started by asking a variety of individuals a simple question: "Do you believe we all have superpowers?" I thought the answer would be immediate. This was immediately followed by, "Then what is yours?" When I asked these questions, it was as if they were staring into a mirror fogged by years of self-doubt and routine. What struck me most was that many people struggled to identify more than one gift or superpower. This led me to a realization: I believe we all possess 3-5 gifts and superpowers that we should be able to draw upon when needed. This is more than those I interviewed were able to give me.

This difficulty in self-recognition reminds me of a fascinating study conducted with a company's leadership team. Each leader was asked to write down their perceived gifts or what they believed they were best at. Most of them could only list one or two gifts. In a surprising twist, when the tables were turned, and peers listed each leader's gifts, the results were eye opening. Their peers could easily identify 4-6 unique gifts for each person. This discrepancy highlighted a common truth: we often don't see in ourselves what others see in us.

Reflecting on my own journey, this insight became a pivotal moment. While I can't recall the exact situations, I vividly remember conversations with my wife, sister, and mother, all of whom made similar statements like, "That's because you're a giver." It was a recurring theme that I had never fully acknowledged. A few days later, I woke up with a sudden clarity: one of my superpowers is being a GIVER. This realization was the spark that inspired me to write this book.

Understanding Your Gift

The Concept of "Gift":

Let's take a step back and really look at the concept of a "gift." Your gifts, talents, and superpowers are unique to you. They are the abilities that come so naturally to you that you might not even recognize them as special. It's easy to get caught up in thinking of gifts as flashy or impressive talents. But sometimes, they're the quiet, natural abilities we've been carrying around without even knowing. It's common to overlook our own strengths because they feel like second nature to us. These innate abilities are often things we do effortlessly, without even realizing their significance or the impact they can have on others.

You might dismiss your organizational skills, thinking everyone can manage tasks as efficiently as you do. Or perhaps you underestimate your ability to connect with others, assuming that making people feel comfortable and heard is something everyone can do.

Maybe you're the person who can walk into a room full of strangers and make everyone feel at ease. Or maybe you're someone who's always been able to break down complex problems, turning chaos into clarity. These abilities, no matter how everyday they may seem to you, are what make you stand out.

Here are some examples of gifts and skills that you might possess or see in others:

- Leadership: Guiding and inspiring others towards a common goal.
- Creativity: Ability to think outside the box and come up with innovative solutions.

- Time Management: Organizing and planning how to divide your time between activities.

- Optimism: Hopefulness and confidence about the future.

- Public Speaking: Comfort and effectiveness in speaking to an audience.

- Analytical Thinking: Ability to analyze information and make data-driven decisions.

- Patience: Ability to wait and endure without becoming annoyed or anxious.

- Diligence: Careful and persistent work or effort.

- Adaptability: Ability to adjust to new conditions.

- Empathy: Deep understanding and connection with others' emotions.

- Inspiring: Motivating others to achieve their potential.

- Conflict Resolution: Skillfully navigating and resolving disputes.

- Intuition: The ability to understand something instinctively without the need for conscious reasoning.

- Charisma: Compelling attractiveness or charm that can inspire devotion in others.

- More examples of gifts and superpowers are found at the end of the chapter.

Often, others can see our gifts and superpowers more clearly than we can. They might come to us for advice or help in areas where we excel, even if we don't see those areas as particularly special. This external validation can be a powerful tool in identifying our true gifts and superpowers. By paying attention to what others appreciate about us, we can start to see the patterns and recognize our own strengths.

Understanding your gifts and superpowers is not just about acknowledging what you're good at; it's about realizing the unique ways in which you can contribute to the world. It's about understanding that these abilities are not just ordinary—they are extraordinary, and they are yours to develop and share.

Multiple Gifts/Superpowers and Their Evolution

You may have several superpowers, each a native talent that comes so naturally to you that you might not think about it often. These gifts are an integral part of who you are, embedded in your essence. As children, we might exhibit one specific gift, such as an innate musical ability, a knack for storytelling, or an exceptional talent for problem-solving. As we grow and navigate life's journey, we can discover hidden talents and nurture them into full-fledged gifts and superpowers.

This journey with the GIVER Method is about more than just recognizing the talents you already know you possess. It's about discovering hidden abilities and declaring new ones as you evolve. You are not confined to a single gift; you have a wealth of superpowers waiting to be explored and nurtured. Just as Luke Skywalker in *Star Wars* discovered his connection to the Force, learned to wield it, and ultimately used it to create significant change, you too can have a similar journey of self-discovery and empowerment.

The beauty of this process lies in its constantly evolving nature. Your abilities can strengthen and grow over time. With practice, dedication, and a willingness to push beyond your comfort zone, you can upgrade these gifts into true superpowers. You can become an expert in your field, honing your skills to a level where you can teach and inspire others. Think of your journey as a continuous cycle of discovery and development. As you uncover new talents, you can integrate them into your life, enhancing your capacity to give and make a difference.

The Importance of External Perspectives

We're often too close to ourselves to see the full picture. It's like trying to read a map with your nose pressed against it. That's why feedback from others is so important. When we hear how others describe our strengths, we often learn something surprising about ourselves.

Listening to different perspectives is crucial in our journey to becoming a GIVER. It's not just about getting feedback but truly valuing and embracing different viewpoints. Often, feedback tends to be positive, offering praise and encouragement. While this builds confidence, it doesn't always lead to meaningful change or growth. To evolve and develop our gifts into superpowers, we need to seek out and appreciate the deeper insights that come from diverse perspectives.

It reminds me of a quote I once came across by Steve Goodier that says, "We don't get harmony when everybody sings the same note." True growth isn't about staying in our own bubble. This resonates deeply with the idea that true growth and innovation stem from a chorus of different voices, each contributing a unique perspective. Harmony, in this sense, is about the blend of diverse thoughts and ideas creating something more beautiful and complex than any single note could achieve on its own.

A common expression is that, "It is not the strongest or the most intelligent who will survive but those who can best manage change." This quote underscores the importance of adaptability and openness to new ideas. In our personal and professional lives, the ability to manage change and embrace different viewpoints is often what sets us apart and drives us forward. It's not just about holding onto what we know but about being willing to learn, adapt, and grow from the insights others offer.

Developing perspective-taking skills can significantly impact our personal and professional relationships. It strengthens our ability to empathize, builds trust, and creates a sense of compassion and connection. When we actively listen and seek to understand others' viewpoints, we build stronger relationships based on mutual respect and understanding. This not only enhances our ability to connect with others but also fosters a collaborative and inclusive environment where everyone feels valued.

Perspective-taking encourages self-reflection and self-awareness, fostering empathy and understanding. It challenges us to question our own assumptions and biases. By embracing different perspectives, we open ourselves up to new possibilities and ideas, making us more adaptable and resilient in the face of change.

Incorporating perspective-taking into our daily lives involves intentional practice. This can include actively listening to others, asking open-ended questions, and reflecting on our own emotions and reactions. In personal relationships, perspective-taking helps us navigate conflicts, understand our loved ones better, and build stronger connections. In professional settings, it enhances communication, fosters collaboration, and promotes a more inclusive and productive work environment.

As you continue on your journey to become a GIVER, remember the power of external perspectives. Embrace the diverse viewpoints around you, seek out feedback that challenges and inspires you, and cultivate the skills of empathy and perspective-taking.

Overcoming Obstacles

We all experience moments of doubt, that little voice whispering, "Who do you think you are?" It's in these moments that we need to remember: doubt is part of the process.

> If you're feeling uncertain, it means you're stepping into something new—just like I did when I first started asking those around me what my strengths really were.

Self-doubt, often referred to as "imposter syndrome," can significantly hinder self-discovery and the recognition of your gifts and superpowers. This feeling of inadequacy or fear of being exposed as a fraud is surprisingly common, even among the most accomplished individuals. It's important to understand that feeling like an imposter means you are pushing your boundaries. It's a natural part of stepping out of your comfort zone and striving for excellence.

A quick story to set the scene. I have had the privilege of attending events and masterminds with people who have achieved remarkable success—Olympic medalists, published authors, communication experts, and influential business leaders. Despite their achievements, these individuals often express feelings of self-doubt and imposter syndrome. What stands out is their humility and their willingness to give and support others. They seek help and advice just like anyone else, reminding us that self-doubt doesn't diminish their accomplishments; it highlights their desire to keep growing.

Realizing that everyone feels self-doubt at times can be incredibly empowering. It shows that you are not alone in your struggles. Embrace this feeling as a sign that you are on the right path, challenging yourself to reach new heights. When you acknowledge and accept your self-doubt, you can use it as a motivator rather than a barrier. Surround yourself with supportive and like-minded individuals who uplift and encourage you. Remember, even those who seem confident and successful have their moments of doubt. The key is to keep moving forward, leveraging your unique gifts and superpowers to create a positive impact in the world.

Celebrate your achievements, no matter how small they may seem. Each step forward is a testament to your resilience and determination. By shifting your mindset and viewing self-doubt as a part of the growth process, you can break free from its limitations and fully embrace your journey to becoming a GIVER.

Visualization Exercise

Here is a visualization exercise that may help in identifying the initial gifts and superpowers you will be focusing on throughout each of the following chapters.

Visualization is a powerful tool for identifying and understanding your strengths and how you can use them in different contexts. Take some time to imagine your ideal work environment or situation and analyze the skills and strengths you would use.

Setting the Scene: Close your eyes and picture your ideal work environment. Where are you? What does the space look like? Who is there with you?

Activities and Roles: Imagine the activities you are engaged in. What tasks are you performing? What role do you play in this environment?

Utilizing Strengths: As you visualize yourself in this ideal setting, think about the skills and strengths you are using. Are you leading a team, solving complex problems, creating innovative solutions, or providing support and guidance?

Emotional State: Pay attention to how you feel in this ideal situation. Are you confident, energized, and fulfilled? What aspects of this environment contribute to these positive feelings?

Applying Insights: Reflect on how the strengths and skills you identified in this visualization can be applied to your current life. What changes can you make to better align your work and personal life with this ideal vision?

Encouragement to Keep a Journal

Throughout this book, continue to use your journal to document your reflections, insights, and progress. Regular journaling will help you stay connected to your journey, track your growth, and reinforce the development of your gifts and superpowers. Remember, self-reflection is a powerful tool for personal and professional growth. By taking the time to reflect regularly, you are investing in your journey to becoming a GIVER and creating a meaningful, impactful life.

Optional Resource

For a more structured approach to uncovering your strengths, consider the StrengthsFinder 2.0 assessment by Gallup. This tool provides detailed insights into your top strengths, offering a comprehensive understanding of your natural talents and how they manifest in your behavior and interactions.

Benefits of StrengthsFinder 2.0:

- Detailed Insights: Gain a deeper understanding of your natural talents.

- Actionable Advice: Receive practical suggestions on how to apply your strengths in various aspects of your life.

- Enhanced Self-Awareness: Develop a clearer sense of your strengths, boosting your confidence and helping you to focus on what you do best.

You can purchase the StrengthsFinder 2.0 assessment online through Gallup's official website or major online retailers like Amazon. You can also check with your workplace or local library to see if they offer access to this resource. Incorporating the insights from StrengthsFinder 2.0 into your journey with the GIVER Method can enhance your understanding of your unique gifts and empower you to make a greater impact in both your personal and professional life.

Combining Reflections and Insights

First, take a moment to synthesize all the information you've gathered from your self-reflection exercises, peer feedback, and worksheets. This process will help you gain a clearer picture of your gifts and superpowers.

Consider the journey you've taken to discover these gifts and superpowers. What patterns have emerged? What insights have surprised you? Reflect on how this process has changed your understanding of your abilities and potential.

Gift Sharing Experiment

Now that you have a clearer understanding of your gifts, it's time to put them into action. Engaging in a Gift Sharing Experiment will help you see the real-world impact of your talents.

Choose a Specific Gift: Select one of the gifts or superpowers from your list that you feel particularly confident about or excited to share.

Offer Your Expertise: Find a way to share this gift with others. This could be helping a colleague with a project, mentoring someone, volunteering your skills to a community organization, or creating a small project that showcases your talent.

Reflect on the Experience: After sharing your gift, take some time to reflect on the experience. How did it feel to use your gift in a meaningful way? What feedback did you receive? What impact did you notice on those you helped?

Long-Term Goal Setting

To ensure continuous growth and the effective utilization of your gifts, set long-term goals that align with your strengths and aspirations.

Identify Growth Opportunities: Consider areas where you can further develop and refine your gifts and superpowers. This might involve taking a course, attending workshops, or seeking out new challenges that push you to expand your abilities.

Seek Mentorship: Look for mentors or role models who excel in areas related to your gifts. Their guidance and experience can provide valuable insights and support as you continue to grow.

Incorporate Gifts into Daily Routine: Find ways to integrate your gifts into your everyday life. Whether it's through your professional work, personal projects, or community involvement, regularly using your strengths will help you stay connected to your true potential.

Set Specific Goals: Write down specific, measurable, achievable, relevant, and time-bound (SMART) goals related to your gifts and superpowers..

- Specific: Define clear and precise goals. Ask yourself: What exactly do I want to achieve? Why is this goal important? Who is involved?

- Measurable: Determine how you will measure progress and success. Consider: What metrics or indicators will track my progress? How will I know when I've achieved my goal?

- Achievable: Ensure your goals are realistic and attainable. Reflect on: Do I have the necessary resources and skills to achieve this goal? What steps will I take to reach this goal?

- Relevant: Align your goals with your overall vision and objectives. Ask: How does this goal contribute to my personal and professional growth? Why is this goal relevant to my overall journey as a GIVER?

- Time-bound: Set a clear timeline for achieving your goals. Define: When will I start working on this goal? What is the deadline for achieving this goal? Are there any milestones or checkpoints along the way?

Example of a SMART Goal for Personal Life

- Specific: I will use my gift of cooking to prepare and host a dinner for my friends and family.

- Measurable: I will prepare a three-course meal for 10 people and gather feedback from at least 5 of them about the food and the experience.

- Achievable: I will dedicate one hour each evening for two weeks to plan the menu, shop for ingredients, and practice cooking each dish.

- Relevant: This goal will help me enhance my cooking skills, build confidence in hosting events, and create memorable experiences for my loved ones.

- Time-bound: I will host the dinner within one month from today.

Example of a SMART Goal for Professional Life

- Specific: I will create and publish a series of three blog posts on effective time management strategies.

- Measurable: I will track the number of views, comments, and shares for each blog post.

- Achievable: I will allocate two hours each week to research and write the blog posts.

- Relevant: This goal will help me establish myself as an expert in time management and provide valuable content to my audience.

- Time-bound: I will publish the first blog post by the end of the first month, the second by the end of the second month, and the third by the end of the third month.

Reflection Questions

Use these questions to guide your reflections and deepen your understanding of your gifts and superpowers:

- What new insights have you gained about your gifts and superpowers through this process?
- How do the perspectives of others align or differ from your self-assessment?
- What actions can you take to better utilize your gifts and powers in your personal and professional life?
- How did sharing your gift impact you and those around you?

BONUS: Exploring Your Gifts and Superpowers

The following list is not exhaustive but serves as a starting point to help you identify and reflect on your own talents and strengths. Remember, this is a personal journey, and your gifts may differ from those listed here. Embrace the process of discovery and trust that your unique abilities are valuable and impactful.

Gifts and Superpowers

This list can help you to identify, nurture, and share your unique gifts and superpowers in both personal and professional contexts. Use it as a guide to start recognizing the talents and strengths that set you apart and enable you to make a meaningful impact in your world.

Gifts and Skills

1. Creativity: Ability to think outside the box and come up with innovative solutions.

2. Empathy: Understanding and sharing the feelings of others.

3. Leadership: Guiding and inspiring others towards a common goal.

4. Communication: Effectively conveying ideas and information.

5. Problem-Solving: Analyzing situations and finding effective solutions.

6. Time Management: Organizing and planning how to divide your time between activities.

7. Project Management: Planning, executing, and overseeing projects to ensure they are completed

efficiently.

8. Event Planning: Coordinating and organizing events or activities.

9. Teaching: Ability to educate and mentor others.

10. Technical Skills: Proficiency in specific technologies or methodologies.

11. Public Speaking: Comfort and effectiveness in speaking to an audience.

12. Writing: Ability to express ideas clearly and engagingly through written words.

13. Negotiation: Ability to reach mutually beneficial agreements.

14. Artistic Ability: Skill in creating visual art, music, or other creative works.

15. Analytical Thinking: Ability to analyze information and make data-driven decisions.

Character Traits

1. Resilience: Ability to recover from setbacks and keep going.

2. Patience: Ability to wait and endure without becoming annoyed or anxious.

3. Compassion: Deep awareness of and sympathy for others' suffering.

4. Integrity: Adherence to moral and ethical principles.

5. Courage: Ability to confront fear, pain, or adversity.

6. Humility: Having a modest view of one's importance.

7. Diligence: Careful and persistent work or effort.

8. Confidence: Belief in oneself and one's abilities.

9. Adaptability: Ability to adjust to new conditions.

10. Gratitude: Being thankful and showing appreciation.

11. Dependability: Being reliable and trustworthy.

12. Optimism: Hopefulness and confidence about the future.

13. Curiosity: Eagerness to learn and understand new things.

14. Honesty: Being truthful and sincere.

15. Kindness: Being friendly, generous, and considerate.

Real Superpowers

1. Empathy: Deep understanding and connection with others' emotions.

2. Intuition: The ability to understand something instinctively without the need for conscious

reasoning.

3. Visionary Thinking: Seeing beyond the present and envisioning future poss§ibilities.

4. Healing: Helping others recover emotionally or physically.

5. Inspiring: Motivating others to achieve their potential.

6. Networking: Building and maintaining relationships that are mutually beneficial.

7. Transformational Leadership: Inspiring and motivating change in others.

8. Conflict Resolution: Skillfully navigating and resolving disputes.

9. Mindfulness: Maintaining a moment-by-moment awareness of thoughts, feelings, and surroundings.

10. Strategic Thinking: Planning for the future with clear goals and well-thought-out plans.

11. Adaptability: Quickly adjusting to new conditions or environments.

12. Charisma: Compelling attractiveness or charm that can inspire devotion in others.

13. Persistence: Continuing firmly on a course of action despite difficulty or opposition.

14. Creativity: Producing original and valuable ideas.

15. Compassionate Listening: Giving others your full attention and understanding.

Examples of Alignment (Skills to Character Traits to Real Superpowers)

Gift: Empathy

- Skill: Active Listening, Emotional Intelligence
- Character Trait: Compassion, Patience
- Real Superpower: Deep Understanding and Connection with Others' Emotions

Gift: Leadership

- Skill: Public Speaking, Team Management
- Character Trait: Integrity, Confidence
- Real Superpower: Transformational Leadership

Gift: Creativity

- Skill: Artistic Ability, Innovative Problem-Solving
- Character Trait: Curiosity, Optimism
- Real Superpower: Visionary Thinking

Exercises and Actionable Content

You can access the Chapter 2 worksheets by going to www.
thegivermethod.com/Chapter-2-worksheets

Chapter 3:
Becoming a Gift Giver

Developing Your Unique Gifts and Superpowers

"The meaning of life is to find your gift. The purpose of life is to give it away."
- Pablo Picasso

Reaching This Milestone on Your Journey

Making it to Chapter 3 means you've already committed to a journey that many begin but few truly stick with. Think about that for a moment. It's easy to open a book and maybe skim through a few pages with good intentions, but the real work—the work you're doing—takes effort. You're here because you've decided to do more than just read. You've chosen to uncover what lies beneath the surface and become a GIVER.

Reflect on the gifts and superpowers you listed. Are they truly your superpowers? Often, skills, talents, and gifts you discover are indicators pointing to deeper, more impactful gifts. Sometimes, what we initially identify as a gift can lead us to discover a more profound capability and even a superpower. For instance, my wife initially identified time management and project management as her superpowers. While both are valuable, we later realized her true gift was party/event planning and execution, which stemmed from those skills. This realization came from observing her in action, seeing how her meticulous organization and strategic planning culminated in creating memorable and flawlessly executed events. While her time management and project skills were impressive, they were just a piece of the puzzle that was her overall capability and unique gift.

As you move forward, keep in mind that the goal is not just to identify your gifts but to develop them into powerful superpowers that you can use to make a difference. This chapter will guide you through embracing and showcasing your gifts, overcoming any fears you might have about sharing them, and building the confidence to use them effectively in both your personal and professional life.

By staying committed to this process, you are setting yourself up for profound personal growth and the ability to make a meaningful impact on those around you. The effort you put in now will pay dividends in the future, as you unlock your full potential and become a true GIVER.

Acknowledging Struggles: Overcoming Self-Doubt and Peer Perceptions

If there's one thing I've learned, it's that self-doubt has a sneaky way of creeping in just when you think you've found your stride. Maybe you've felt it already—those whispers that say, "Am I really good enough?" or "Do I even have anything special to offer?" Trust me, those thoughts are normal, but they don't have to define you. Self-doubt and imposter syndrome are common obstacles on this journey. These feelings of inadequacy and fear of being exposed as a fraud can really undermine your confidence.

I can't count how many times I've been surrounded by people I admire—people whose achievements are staggering—and felt a pang of imposter syndrome. But here's what I've learned: even the most successful among us wrestle with self-doubt. The key is to recognize it for what it is—fear disguised as self-preservation. It's a barrier that pops up when you're on the verge of growth. So, when you feel it, take it as a sign that you're exactly where you need to be.

What matters is how you respond. Are you going to let that doubt keep you silent? Or are you going to push through and share your voice? Your opinions, your gifts— they matter. Silence may feel like the safer route, but staying quiet only guarantees missed opportunities to grow and connect. Start small: share your thoughts with a trusted friend, or speak up in a meeting. The more you do it, the easier it becomes.

So, how do you combat self-doubt and boost your self-confidence?

Here are some strategies to consider:

Recognize That Everyone Has Opinions, Including You: Your perspective is valuable. Just because someone else has a different viewpoint doesn't mean yours is less valid. Everyone's experiences shape their opinions, and yours are just as important.

Don't Be Afraid of Judgment from Others: Fear of judgment can paralyze you. Understand that people will always have opinions, but that doesn't mean you should let those opinions dictate your actions. Focus on your goals and what you believe in.

Having an Opinion is Always Better Than Staying Silent: Contributing your thoughts and ideas is crucial. Even if your opinion isn't always well-received, it shows that you are engaged and willing to take a stand. Silence may feel safe, but it often leads to missed opportunities for growth and connection.

Preface Your Statements with "In My Opinion": This can help ease the pressure of feeling like you need to have all the answers. It acknowledges that you are sharing a personal perspective, which can make it easier to speak up and share your thoughts.

If you struggle with reconciling others' perceptions of you, keep these points in mind:

Negative Feedback Can Be an Opportunity for Growth: Instead of viewing criticism as a personal attack, see it as a chance to improve. Constructive feedback, even if it's hard to hear, can provide valuable insights into areas where you can grow.

Focus on Feedback from Trusted Sources: Not all feedback is created equal. Seek input from people who know you well and have your best interests at heart. These individuals can provide balanced, honest feedback that is more likely to be constructive and helpful.

Not Everyone Will Like You, and That's Okay: It's impossible to please everyone. Accepting this can be liberating. Focus on being true to yourself and your values, and let go of the need for universal approval.

Develop Self-Compassion: Be kind to yourself. Understand that everyone makes mistakes and has moments of doubt. Treat yourself with the same kindness and understanding that you would offer a friend in a similar situation.

Celebrate Your Achievements: Take time to acknowledge your successes, no matter how small they may seem. Celebrating your wins can boost your confidence and remind you of your capabilities.

Seek Support: Surround yourself with supportive people who encourage you and believe in your abilities. This can make a significant difference in overcoming self-doubt.

Reframe Negative Thoughts: Challenge negative self-talk by focusing on how you can approach challenges differently and build confidence. Reframing your thoughts can shift your mindset from self-doubt to self-belief.

Set Realistic Goals: Break down your goals into manageable tasks and tackle them incrementally. Achieving small milestones can build momentum and confidence over time.

Don't Shoot Yourself Down: It's important to approach this process with an optimistic and open mindset. Avoid the temptation to dismiss your abilities or compare yourself to others. Everyone has unique gifts, and yours are no less valuable just because they might be different from someone else's. Embrace the process with self-compassion and curiosity.

Turn to a Friend or Loved One for Assistance: Sometimes, it can be challenging to see our own strengths clearly. If you're struggling to identify your gifts, don't hesitate to ask for help. Reach out to friends, family members, or colleagues who know you well. They can offer valuable insights and perspectives that you might not see in yourself. They may point out strengths and talents that you take for granted or haven't fully recognized.

Reflect on Past Experiences: Think about times in your life when you felt particularly engaged, fulfilled, or successful. What were you doing? What skills or qualities were you using? Reflecting on these moments can help you identify patterns and uncover your hidden gifts.

Consider Feedback You've Received: Reflect on feedback you've received from others in the past. Have people consistently praised you for certain skills or qualities? These recurring compliments can be strong indicators of your gifts and superpowers. Pay attention to what others see in you, as this external perspective can be incredibly revealing.

Look at What Comes Naturally to You: Your gifts and superpowers are often things that come naturally to you— activities or skills that you find easy or enjoyable. What do you do effortlessly that others might find challenging? What activities make you lose track of time because you are so immersed in them? These are clues to your natural talents.

Engage in Self-Reflection Exercises: Use the self-reflection exercises provided in the worksheets to guide your thinking. These exercises are designed to help you dig deeper into your experiences, strengths, and passions. Take your time with these exercises, and be honest with yourself. The more you reflect, the more you will discover.

Embrace the Journey of Discovery: Identifying your gifts is a journey, not a destination. Be patient with yourself and enjoy the process of self-discovery. Your understanding of your gifts may evolve over time, and that's perfectly okay. The important thing is to start exploring and recognizing the unique qualities that make you who you are.

Remember, everyone has gifts and superpowers. By taking the time to reflect, seek input from others, and use the tools provided, you will discover the unique talents that you possess. These gifts are the foundation of your journey to becoming a GIVER, and embracing them is the first step toward making a meaningful impact in your life and the lives of others.

Developing Your Gifts and Superpowers

Nurturing Gifts

In Chapter 2, you began the process of identifying your gifts. Now, it's time to nurture them—to turn them into true superpowers that can change your life and the lives of those around you. Think of it like planting seeds. You've already done the hard work of identifying what you're working with. Now, it's time to cultivate those seeds into something extraordinary.

Here's what I've found works best:

Set Clear Goals: It's time to reinforce that point because having clear goals is crucial for your growth. Knowing exactly how you want to grow and what you want to achieve with your gifts provides direction and motivation. For instance, if your gift is public speaking, you might set a goal to deliver a speech at a local event within the next three months. Start by preparing your speech, practice in front of friends or family, and seek feedback to refine your delivery. Each small milestone you reach is a step towards your ultimate goal. Celebrate these achievements—they are proof of your progress.

Daily Journaling and Weekly Reflections: Use the provided templates to document your journey. Daily journaling helps you reflect on how you applied your gifts and superpowers each day, what you learned, and any challenges you faced. Weekly reflections give you a broader view, allowing you to evaluate your overall progress, identify patterns, and set new goals. This practice keeps you focused, motivated, and aware of your growth.

Exposure: Spend time with people who excel in the areas you wish to improve. This could involve shadowing a mentor, attending workshops led by experts, or participating in professional groups. Observing and interacting with skilled individuals provides valuable insights and inspiration. Ask questions, seek advice, and learn from their experiences. For example, if you want to improve your leadership skills, find a mentor within your organization or industry. Explain your goals and ask if you can shadow them for a period. Regular meetings to discuss your observations, ask questions, and receive feedback can be incredibly beneficial.

Education: Actively seek knowledge through books, courses, and seminars related to your gifts and superpowers. Education expands your understanding and equips you with new techniques and strategies. Choose resources that align with your goals and learning style. For instance, if your gift is creative writing, enroll in a writing workshop or read books on storytelling and narrative techniques.

Environment: Find or create a supportive environment where you can practice and grow without fear of failure. Surround yourself with encouraging people who believe in your potential and provide constructive feedback. This could be a study group, a professional network, or a supportive community like the GIVER Method. A hopeful environment fosters experimentation and learning, allowing you to develop your gifts and superpowers with confidence.

Experience: Gain practical experience by using your gifts regularly, even if you start small. The more you practice, the more you improve. Look for opportunities to apply your gifts in various settings—volunteer projects, side gigs, or personal challenges. For instance, if your gift is teaching, offer to tutor students or lead a workshop in your community. Practical experience helps you refine your skills, build confidence, and discover new ways to utilize your gifts and superpowers.

Evaluation: Seek honest feedback from trusted individuals to understand your strengths and areas for improvement. Feedback provides a different perspective and helps you see blind spots. Choose people who are knowledgeable and supportive, such as mentors, colleagues, or friends. Ask specific questions about your performance and be open to constructive criticism. For example, after giving a presentation, ask for feedback on your delivery, content, and audience engagement. Use this input to make adjustments and enhance your abilities.

It's the daily, intentional practice that turns a gift into a superpower. For me, I've spent years honing my ability to simplify complex problems, breaking them down into digestible pieces. It didn't happen overnight. It was a process of trial and error, feedback, and continuous improvement. But each time I used that gift, it became sharper, more defined. The same will happen for you, as long as you're willing to put in the work.

Incorporating Gifts and Superpowers

One of my gifts and superpowers is my ability to fall asleep in an instant and to wake up as early as I want to get more done in the day. Some people think I am crazy for waking up at 3:00am. This means I am usually at my office by 4:00am at the latest. People ask why I do this and I always reply with, "That's Jake Time." I have no one else around, and I have the office to myself for three-plus hours. "Jake Time" is Self-Compassion time. I am able to read, meditate/pray/ponder, journal, reflect, and plan my day. It is what puts me into the right frame of thinking for the day. Now, you don't have to wake up at 3:00am to show self-compassion, but you should block out daily time to do so.

Using your gifts and superpowers isn't just about big moments. It's about weaving them into the fabric of your daily life—at home, at work, in your community. It's about using what makes you uniquely you to create something meaningful in every interaction. By actively using your unique strengths, you not only enhance your own life but also create positive chain reactions that benefit those around you.

Take a moment to think about your day-to-day life. Where can you infuse your gifts? If you're someone who thrives on connection, how can you use that to strengthen your relationships at home? Maybe it's as simple as being more present during conversations or planning small moments of joy for your family. If your gift is problem-solving, how can you apply that to your workplace to streamline processes or offer support to a colleague?

> Your gifts are not meant to sit on the sidelines,
> waiting for the perfect moment. They're meant to
> be in motion, shaping the world around you,
> one small act at a time.

Here are some examples of how to incorporate your gifts and superpowers daily:

Personal Life: Use your gifts and superpowers in everyday interactions and activities to enhance your personal relationships and daily experiences. For example, if your gift is empathy, practice active listening with friends and family. Show genuine interest in their thoughts and feelings, and respond with understanding and compassion. This strengthens your relationships and builds trust.

If you have a creative talent, such as writing or painting, incorporate it into your routine. Keep a journal, write short stories, or create art projects with your children. This not only nurtures your gift but also brings joy and fulfillment to your daily life. If you're skilled at problem-solving, apply this gift to everyday challenges. Whether it's planning a family vacation, organizing a home project, or helping a friend with a dilemma, use your analytical skills to find effective solutions.

If teaching is your strength, share your knowledge with those around you. Help your children with their homework, organize a book club, or offer to teach a skill to a friend. Teaching not only benefits others but also reinforces your own knowledge and abilities.

Professional Life: Integrating your gifts and superpowers into your work can enhance your performance, build your reputation, and create a more fulfilling career. For instance, if you're a natural leader, look for opportunities to lead projects or mentor colleagues. Take initiative, guide your team, and support others in their professional growth. Your leadership can inspire and motivate others, fostering a beneficial and productive work environment.

If you excel in communication, use this gift to improve your workplace interactions. Clearly articulate ideas, actively participate in meetings, and facilitate effective communication among your team. Strong communication skills can lead to better collaboration and successful outcomes.

If you have a knack for innovation, apply this gift to your work projects. Propose new ideas, streamline processes, and find creative solutions to challenges. Your innovative approach can drive progress and set you apart as a valuable asset to your organization.

If empathy is your strength, use it to build strong relationships with colleagues and clients. Understand their needs and perspectives, and provide support and assistance. Empathy can lead to better teamwork, client satisfaction, and a positive work atmosphere.

Community Involvement: Volunteer your time and talents in your community to make a positive impact and build meaningful connections. For instance, use your skills where they can make a difference. If you're good at organizing events, help plan community activities or fundraisers.

If you have medical training, volunteer at health clinics or support groups. Offer to mentor young people or those new to your field by providing guidance. Mentoring can have a lasting impact on individuals and contribute to the growth of your community.

If you excel in public speaking, volunteer to give talks or presentations at local schools, community centers, or organizations. Use your gift and superpowers to educate, inspire, and engage your audience on important topics.

If you are passionate about a cause, use your advocacy skills to promote awareness and drive change. Join community groups, participate in campaigns, and use your voice to support initiatives that align with your values.

Overcoming Fear

Let's talk about fear. Not just self-doubt, but the kind of fear that stops you from stepping out and using your gifts in the first place. Fear is different from self-doubt and imposter syndrome. While self-doubt makes you question whether you have the gift or if anyone would want it, and imposter syndrome makes you feel like a fraud despite your accomplishments, fear is about the act of stepping out and actually using your gifts and superpowers. It's the barrier you feel when you're about to take action. Understanding this distinction is crucial because it allows you to tackle each challenge appropriately and helps you recognize that overcoming fear is a key step in actively using and showcasing your talents.

I know that fear all too well. It's the hesitation before offering to help someone when you're not sure if your help will be wanted. It's the worry that if you show your true self, you'll somehow fall short. But here's what I've come to understand: the real tragedy isn't in failing; it's in never trying at all. Every time you take action, you build confidence, and with each step, fear begins to lose its grip.

Start small. Begin by sharing your gifts in low-stakes environments to build confidence gradually. Maybe it's as simple as helping a friend solve a problem or sharing an idea in a small group. Each time you put your gifts into action, you'll feel a little more comfortable. And before you know it, fear will no longer be what's holding you back. This approach lets you ease into using your talents without the pressure of high expectations or significant consequences.

Share your gifts with close family, friends, and other supportive and encouraging people. Whether it's cooking a special meal, offering advice, or sharing a creative project, your loved ones can provide feedback and positive reinforcement. Mentors and coaches (experienced professionals who aid you in your career or personal development) can guide you in similar ways and offer constructive feedback. You can also join local clubs, groups, or organizations where you can practice your skills in a friendly and supportive setting. This could be a hobby group, a volunteer organization, or a local workshop. You can also use social media or online forums to share your talents with a broader audience. These platforms offer a relatively low-pressure way to showcase your skills and receive feedback from people who share your interests.

Focus on the value your gifts and superpowers can bring. Concentrate on the positive impact your gifts and superpowers can have on others. Shifting your focus from your fears to the benefits you can provide helps to reduce anxiety and build motivation. For example, if you have a talent for teaching, consider how your lessons can empower and educate your students. Embrace the satisfaction that comes from knowing you are making a difference. You can also consider the long-term impact of your gifts and superpowers. By sharing your talents, you contribute to a legacy of positive change and inspiration that can influence future generations.

Visualization exercises, or mentally rehearsing successful scenarios, can also reduce anxiety. Close your eyes and visualize yourself confidently sharing your gifts and superpowers in different situations. Imagine the positive reactions and outcomes, such as receiving praise, making a meaningful impact, or achieving your goals. Make your visualization as detailed as possible. Picture the environment, the people involved, and your actions. Focus on the feelings of satisfaction, pride, and accomplishment that come with successfully using your gifts and superpowers. Incorporate these exercises into your daily routine to reinforce positive thinking and build confidence over time.

Embrace failure as a natural part of growth and learning. Understand that making mistakes is an opportunity to improve and refine your skills. Set realistic goals by breaking them down into smaller, manageable steps. Practice self-compassion by being kind to yourself and recognizing that fear is a common human experience.

I have learned the value of mindful meditation over the years. For some reason, around the age of 37, my brain discovered this thing called "anxiety." Not sure if you've heard of it or not (haha, just kidding). When this anxiety hits me, it is borderline crippling. Over time, I would find ways to work it out when they happened, but they would still occur regularly. Once I started doing mindful meditation and, in some cases, breath-work, I found that these anxiety attacks became farther apart. Now, they haven't gone away completely, but I have far fewer of them, and when they do come on, I am able to relieve myself of them faster using this practice.

I'm not sure if you are like me, but at the end of the day, my mind can be racing with everything that happened that day. Between work, wife, boys, dog, church, family, and friends, my life can get very busy. So busy that I felt it was a great idea to add writing a book to it. For years, I struggled to fall asleep because my mind would be so caught up on the items of the day or thinking and worrying about things for tomorrow. I found that journaling was one of the best ways for me to calm my mind and allow me to think more clearly.

Supportive Feedback

Seeking and reflecting on supportive feedback helps you gain new perspectives, identify areas for improvement, and reinforce your strengths. Here's how to effectively seek and utilize supportive feedback:

Choosing Trusted Advisors

Feedback should come from people who understand your goals, respect your journey, and can offer honest, constructive criticism. Think about who in your life genuinely understands your aspirations and has a clear perspective on your abilities. This could include mentors, colleagues, friends, family members, or professional coaches. Consider whether these individuals have the knowledge or experience to give valuable feedback in the areas you wish to improve. Ensure you have a relationship of mutual trust and respect with these advisors, as their feedback should come from a place of wanting to see you succeed.

Asking Specific Questions

General inquiries often lead to vague responses, while targeted questions can provide deeper insights. Framing your questions effectively is crucial to gaining valuable feedback. Focus on improvement by asking questions that highlight areas where you want to grow. For example, you might ask, "What do you think I could improve on in my communication skills?" Seek feedback on how you are currently using your strengths, asking questions like, "How do you see me utilizing my leadership skills effectively?" Encourage honesty by letting your advisors know that you value their honest opinion and are open to candid feedback.

Other example questions include:

"What is one area where you think I could improve?"

"Can you give me an example of how I've effectively used my analytical skills?"

"How do you perceive my progress in achieving my goals?"

Reflecting on Feedback

Once you've received feedback, take the time to reflect on it and consider how it fits into your growth plan. Reflection helps you internalize the feedback and develop actionable steps to enhance your skills and abilities. Here's how to reflect:

Review and Digest: Carefully read or listen to the feedback you've received. Take notes on key points and insights. (Example: "After receiving feedback from my mentor, I noticed they mentioned my presentation skills need refinement.")

Identify Patterns: Look for recurring themes or suggestions across different feedback sources. This can highlight significant areas for improvement or consistent strengths. (Example: "Both my mentor and a colleague suggested I work on making my presentations more engaging.")

Incorporate Feedback: Think about how you can integrate the feedback into your growth plan. This might involve setting new goals, adopting different strategies, or seeking further education or practice in certain areas. (Example: "I will enroll in a public speaking course and practice my presentations with a friend to get more comfortable.")

Plan Action Steps: Develop a clear plan to address the feedback. Set specific, actionable steps you can take to improve and enhance your performance. (Example: "My goal is to improve my presentation skills within the next three months by completing the course and practicing weekly.")

Gift Sharing Action Plan

Creating a Gift Sharing Action Plan involves identifying opportunities, brainstorming creative ways to share your gifts and superpowers, and setting SMART goals to ensure successful implementation. Here's a step-by-step guide to help you understand and develop each component of your plan:

Identify Opportunities

The first step is to identify specific situations where you can share your gifts and superpowers. This involves looking at different aspects of your life and recognizing where your talents can be most impactful. Consider opportunities in your personal life, professional environment, and community involvement. For example, if your gift is public speaking, opportunities might include giving a presentation at work, speaking at a community event, or leading a workshop.

Personal Life: Look for opportunities within your family and social circles. For example, you might:

- Offer to organize family events or gatherings if you have a talent for event planning.

- Provide tutoring or mentorship to younger family members or friends if you excel in a particular subject or skill.

- Share your creative talents, like painting or music, during social get-togethers or community events.

Professional Life: Identify situations at work where you can apply your gifts and superpowers to benefit your team and organization. Examples include:

- Leading a project or initiative that aligns with your strengths.

- Conducting a workshop or training session to share your expertise with colleagues.

- Volunteering for cross-functional teams where your skills can bridge gaps and create synergy.

Community Involvement: Engage with local organizations or groups where your talents can make a difference. Consider:

- Volunteering for community events or causes that align with your passions.

- Offering free classes or workshops at local community centers or schools.

- Participating in local clubs or groups where your skills can contribute to collective goals.

Brainstorm Ideas

Once you've identified opportunities, brainstorm creative ways to showcase your talents. This step builds on the opportunities you've identified by exploring how you can effectively share your gifts and superpowers in these contexts. Think broadly and creatively:

Personal Life

Creative Projects: Use your talents in everyday activities and personal projects.

- If you're good at crafting, make handmade gifts for friends and family. Or teach them how to make these items or gifts themselves.

- If you love cooking, host a dinner party or create a cooking club with friends. Make a family cookbook or share your recipes with others.

- If you have a green thumb, share your gardening tips or produce with neighbors.

Support and Encouragement: Use your empathetic or motivational skills.

- Find training or educational programs that will increase your ability and knowledge on how to help others.

- Be a supportive listener for friends going through tough times. Make sure those who are close to you know they can call you anytime if they need someone to listen.

- Offer to help friends and family set and achieve their personal goals. Ask your family and friends what their goals are and how you can help.

- Use your sense of humor to bring joy and laughter to gatherings. Plan a family event or get together and plan some games or showcase your talents.

Educational Engagement: Share knowledge and skills within your family or close circle.

- Teach your children or siblings new skills, such as playing a musical instrument, cooking, or crafting.
- Start a family book club to discuss interesting books and ideas.
- Lead fitness or mindfulness sessions for your loved ones. Go on group hikes, bike rides, or neighborhood walks.

Professional Life

Content Creation: Create content that highlights your expertise and shares valuable insights with others.

- Write blog posts or articles on topics related to your gifts and superpowers.
- Create videos or podcasts to share your knowledge and experiences.
- Design infographics or visual content that illustrates key concepts and ideas.

Public Speaking: Use your gifts and superpowers in public speaking engagements to reach a broader audience.

- Giving presentations or lectures at conferences, seminars, or community events.
- Host webinars or online workshops to share your knowledge with a global audience.
- Participate in panel discussions or Q&A sessions related to your field of expertise.

Workshops and Classes: Conduct workshops or classes to teach others and share your skills. This can include:

- Organizing in-person or virtual workshops focused on specific skills or topics.
- Offering one-on-one coaching or mentoring sessions.
- Creating online courses or tutorials that provide step-by-step guidance.

Community Involvement

Volunteer Work: Use your skills to benefit local organizations and groups.

- If you're skilled in graphic design, offer to create promotional materials for a local charity.

- If you have a talent for teaching, volunteer to tutor students or lead educational workshops.

- Use your organizational skills to help plan and execute community events.

Local Contributions: Make a positive impact within your community.

- Participate in local clean-up initiatives or environmental projects.

- Share your musical or artistic talents at community events or senior centers.

- Offer free classes or workshops at local community centers or schools.

Collaborative Projects: Engage in collaborative projects that allow you to work with others and leverage your gifts and superpowers. Examples include:

- Partnering with other professionals or organizations on joint initiatives.

- Contributing to community projects or volunteer efforts.

- Collaborating with colleagues on innovative projects that utilize your strengths.

Content Creation Ideas

Leverage your gifts and superpowers to create engaging content across various aspects of your life. Here are some ideas to help you share your talents and make a meaningful impact:

Personal Life

Blog Posts:

- Write about your journey of discovering and developing your gifts and superpowers. Share personal stories, challenges, and triumphs.

- Create posts with tips and advice on how others can discover and nurture similar gifts and superpowers.

- Document personal projects or activities where you've applied your gifts and superpowers, like organizing family events, creating art, or improving your home.

Videos:

- Create video diaries or vlogs that showcase how you use your gifts and superpowers in daily life, such as cooking, crafting, or fitness routines.

- Share tutorials or DIY videos that teach others how to develop similar skills.

- Record personal reflections or motivational talks about the importance of using one's gifts and the impact it has had on your life.

Workshops:

- Host small, informal workshops or gatherings at home to teach friends and family about your gifts and superpowers, like cooking classes, art sessions, or book clubs.

- Organize community meetups where you can share your expertise and learn from others in a supportive environment.

Social Media:

- Use Instagram to share daily snapshots or stories that highlight your gifts and superpowers in action, whether it's through photos, short videos, or live sessions.

- Start a Facebook group where you can connect with others who share similar interests and exchange ideas and support.

- Utilize Pinterest to create boards that inspire others with your projects, ideas, and tutorials.

Professional Life

Blog Posts:

- Write articles on industry-specific applications of your gifts and superpowers, such as leadership strategies, innovative problem-solving, or effective communication techniques.

- Share case studies or success stories where you've used your gifts and superpowers to achieve professional milestones or overcome challenges.

- Offer insights and tips on professional development and how to leverage unique talents in the workplace.

Videos:

- Create instructional videos or webinars that provide valuable knowledge and skills to your professional network.

- Share your expertise through online courses or training sessions that colleagues or industry peers can access.

- Record professional development talks or presentations that showcase your insights and contributions to your field.

Workshops:

- Organize and lead workshops or training sessions within your organization to teach others about your area of expertise.

- Host webinars or virtual workshops to reach a broader audience and share your knowledge with professionals in your industry.

- Participate in or create mastermind groups where you can collaborate with other professionals to share and develop your gifts and superpowers.

Social Media:

- Use LinkedIn to publish articles, share updates, and engage with your professional network about your gifts and how you're using them to make an impact.

- Create a YouTube channel focused on professional growth, offering tutorials, interviews, and discussions on relevant topics.

- Leverage Twitter to share bite-sized insights, tips, and links to longer content, engaging with others in your field and expanding your reach.

By creating diverse content across personal and professional platforms, you can effectively share your gifts and superpowers, inspire others, and build a community around your unique talents. This approach not only enhances your personal growth but also positions you as a valuable contributor in both your personal and professional spheres.

Gift Sharing Matrix

Develop a matrix to organize your gift-sharing efforts, ensuring you make the most impact with your unique talents. This structured approach will help you systematically plan and execute how you share your gifts and superpowers in various areas of your life. Here's how to build your Gift Sharing Matrix:

1. List Your Gifts and Superpowers

Begin by listing each of your identified gifts or superpowers. This will be the foundation of your matrix. Be sure to consider both personal and professional gifts.

Examples:

- Empathy
- Public Speaking
- Artistic Talent
- Problem-Solving
- Leadership

2. Corresponding Actions

For each gift, brainstorm specific actions that allow you to share and utilize these talents. Consider a variety of settings and formats to ensure you're making a broad impact.

Examples:

Empathy: In your personal life you could offer to listen and provide support to friends and family members going through tough times. Write handwritten notes or letters offering encouragement. In your professional life you could lead a peer support group or employee wellness program. Provide one-on-one mentorship to colleagues. For community involvement you could volunteer at local support organizations like crisis hotlines or counseling centers. Organize community meetups focused on mental health awareness.

Public Speaking: In your personal life you could practice giving speeches or presentations at family gatherings or local clubs. Share stories or lessons learned with friends. In your professional life you could lead training sessions, seminars, or team meetings. Present at industry conferences or webinars. For community involvement you could offer to speak at community events, local schools, or non-profit organizations. Host free public speaking workshops.

Artistic Talent: In your personal life you could create and share art pieces with friends and family. Host art nights or craft sessions at home. In your professional life you could use your artistic skills to enhance work presentations or projects. Offer design services to colleagues. For community involvement you could volunteer to teach art classes at community centers or schools. Donate artwork for charity auctions.

Problem-Solving: In your personal life you could help friends and family with planning and organizing tasks. Offer to assist in resolving conflicts or finding creative solutions to personal challenges. In your professional life you could join or lead task forces to address workplace challenges. Develop innovative strategies for projects. For community involvement you could participate in community planning committees or local government advisory boards. Offer consultancy services to local businesses or nonprofits.

Leadership: In your personal life you could take the lead in organizing family events or group outings. Mentor younger family members or friends. In your professional life you could step up for leadership roles in projects and teams. Mentor junior colleagues and provide career guidance. For community involvement you could volunteer for leadership roles in community organizations or non-profits. Organize and lead community service projects.

3. Audiences

Identify who would benefit most from each gift and superpowers. This can include specific groups within your personal, professional, and community spheres.

Examples:

Empathy:

- Personal Life: Friends and family members in need of emotional support.
- Professional Life: Colleagues dealing with work-related stress.
- Community Involvement: Members of support groups or local communities facing hardship.

Public Speaking:

- Personal Life: Social clubs or family gatherings looking for motivational talks.
- Professional Life: Industry peers and colleagues seeking knowledge or inspiration.
- Community Involvement: Local organizations or schools needing guest speakers.

Artistic Talent:

- Personal Life: Friends and family appreciating creative gifts or decorations.

- Professional Life: Teams and clients requiring innovative design work.
- Community Involvement: Community art programs or charity events.

Problem-Solving:

- Personal Life: Friends and family members needing help with planning or organizing.
- Professional Life: Teams tackling complex projects or challenges.
- Community Involvement: Local businesses or non-profits requiring consultancy or strategic planning.

Leadership:

- Personal Life: Family and social groups needing direction or organization.
- Professional Life: Work teams and junior colleagues looking for guidance.
- Community Involvement: Community groups or non-profits seeking leadership and direction.

Building Your Matrix

Here's an example of how your Gift Sharing Matrix might look:

Gift/ Superpower	Actions	Audience
Empathy	- Support friends and family, write encouraging notes, lead peer support groups	- Friends, family, colleagues, support groups
Public Speaking	- Give talks at gatherings, lead training sessions, offer public speaking workshops	- Social clubs, colleagues, community members
Artistic Talent	- Create and share art, enhance presentations, teach community art classes	- Friends, family, colleagues, community centers
Problem-Solving	- Help organize tasks, lead task forces, offer consultancy services	- Family, colleagues, local businesses
Leadership	- Organize events, mentor others, lead community service projects	- Family, social groups, work teams, community

By systematically listing your gifts and superpowers, corresponding actions, and target audiences, you can better visualize and plan how to share your talents effectively. This matrix will serve as a guide to ensure that you are making the most of your gifts and reaching those who can benefit most from them.

Self-Compassion Practices

Engage in daily self-compassion exercises to foster a brighter mindset and enhance your journey towards becoming a GIVER. Self-compassion involves treating yourself with kindness and understanding, particularly during times of struggle or self-doubt. Here are some practical exercises to incorporate into your daily routine:

Morning Affirmations

Start your day with affirmations to set a positive tone and boost your self-confidence. Affirmations are simple, optimistic statements that can help reframe your mindset and reinforce your belief in your abilities and potential. You can use the Daily Journal and Weekly Reflections worksheet to help track progress.

Examples:

- "I am capable and confident in my abilities."
- "I am worthy of success and happiness."
- "Today, I will embrace my gifts and share them with the world."
- "I am growing and improving every day."

How to Practice:

1. Find a quiet place where you can focus without

interruptions.

2.   Choose 3-5 affirmations that resonate with you.

3.   Say each affirmation aloud, with conviction and belief.

4.   Repeat the affirmations several times, visualizing yourself embodying these positive traits and feelings.

Mindful Meditation

Mindful meditation helps you cultivate self-love and acceptance by encouraging you to be present in the moment and observe your thoughts without judgment. This practice can reduce stress and increase your overall sense of well-being.

How to Practice:

1.   Set Aside Time: Dedicate 5-10 minutes each day for meditation.

2.   Find a Comfortable Space: Choose a quiet place where you can sit or lie down comfortably.

3.   Relax: Close your eyes and take a few deep breaths to help you relax.

4.   Focus on Your Breath: Pay attention to the sensation of each inhale and exhale.

5. Acknowledge Thoughts: When thoughts arise, acknowledge them without judgment and gently return your focus to your breath.

6. Incorporate a Mantra: Use a mantra or affirmation related to self-compassion, such as "I am enough" or "I am worthy of love and acceptance."

Identifying Who To Influence and Your Ideal Clients

As you develop your gifts and superpowers, it's important to identify who can benefit most from them. This involves thinking about the individuals or groups you can influence and determining your ideal clients or target audience.

Steps for Identifying Your Audience:

Who Benefits Most: Consider who would gain the most from your gifts and superpowers. These could be colleagues, friends, family, community members, or specific client groups.

Tailor Your Message: Think about how to present your gifts and superpowers in a way that resonates with your target audience. What language, examples, or benefits will make your gifts and superpowers most appealing to them?

Plan for Outreach: Develop a strategy for reaching out to these individuals or groups. This might involve networking, social media engagement, or community involvement.

Example:

- Gift: Leadership

- Audience: Aspiring leaders within your organization.

- Message: Highlight how your leadership can help them grow and develop their own skills.

- Outreach: Offer to mentor new team members or lead a workshop on effective leadership techniques.

Exercises and Actionable Content

This chapter's worksheets and journal exercises contain methods to help you overcome fears, share your gifts, engage in daily self-compassion practices, and more.

You can access the Chapter 3 worksheet by going to www.thegivermethod.com/chapter-3-worksheets

Access The Daily Journal and Weekly Reflections Templates at www.thegivermethod.com/journals

Chapter 4: Influence

Identifying and Tapping Into Influence

"You don't have to be a person of influence to be influential. In fact, the most influential people in my life are probably not even aware of the things they've taught me." – Scott Adams

---

Congratulations! You're making serious strides on your journey to becoming a true GIVER. You've already done the tough work of identifying and refining your gifts—those superpowers that set you apart. By now, you've likely honed in on 3-5 core strengths that shape how you show up in the world. That's no small feat. Recognizing and developing those unique abilities has laid the foundation for what comes next—learning how to wield your influence effectively.

Now, we're moving into the "I" of GIVER—Influence. This is where the real shift happens, where you take your gifts and start applying them in a way that creates meaningful change. It's not enough to know what your gifts are; the next step is understanding how to use them to leave a lasting impact.

I'll never forget the moment when I realized the true power of influence. For over 15 years, I performed improv comedy—not just as a hobby, but as a passion. At my busiest time, I could be doing up to five shows a week. Initially, I did it for fun, enjoying the spotlight and the laughter from the audience. The joy and energy of those moments were incredibly fulfilling.

One of my closest friends, Matt, was diagnosed with cancer. He was in a tough spot, not just physically but financially as well. So, I decided to organize a charity night of comedy for him. It wasn't your typical show. I poured everything into it—getting performers, filling every seat, and making sure the night was perfect. There was a heaviness as the audience came in, but once the show started, something magical happened. For 90 minutes, we weren't in a room filled with worry and pain. We were somewhere else—laughing, smiling, forgetting.

Matt was there, smiling from ear to ear. It was then that I realized my profound influence. I was helping people forget their troubles and bringing joy into their lives, even if just for 60-90 minutes. This experience taught me the true power of influence, a lesson that continues to guide me even though I no longer perform comedy.

Every laugh, every smile, and every moment of joy showed me the positive influence one can have on others. It wasn't just about being on stage; it was about connecting with people on a deeper level and making a difference in their lives. The ability to uplift and inspire, to bring happiness and relief, even temporarily, was a powerful realization.

Reflecting on this, I understood that influence isn't always about grand gestures or widespread recognition. Often, it's the small, personal moments that have the most profound impact. It's about being present, using your gifts and superpowers to serve others, and creating positive change in their lives.

As you dive into this chapter, remember: your influence doesn't have to be grand or visible to everyone. Sometimes, it's those quiet, powerful moments when you uplift someone, when you change the course of their day—or even their life—that hold the most meaning.

Understanding Influence

Influence, within the GIVER Method, is not about being an "influencer" in the modern sense. It's about the positive impact you can have, regardless of recognition. When we talk about influence here, we're referring to your ability to affect the thoughts, feelings, and actions of others in a meaningful way.

Think back to a time when someone's words or actions changed your perspective or inspired you to take action. Maybe it was a teacher who believed in you, a friend who offered support during a tough time, or even a stranger whose kindness brightened your day. That's influence in action, and it's a power we all possess.

The beauty of influence in this context is that it doesn't require a large platform or social media following. It's about the authentic connections we make and the genuine way we show up in our interactions, big and small. Your influence can be as simple as brightening someone's day with a smile or as profound as inspiring a colleague to pursue their dreams.

The Dual Nature of Influence

When I interviewed people while writing this book, one topic came up time and again: influence can go wrong. On almost every call, someone would inevitably comment, "But influence can be used for the wrong reasons." I fully acknowledge that some people may try to influence others for the wrong reasons.

When I asked in those interviews, "How do you ensure you don't fall into the trap of improper influence?" I received some of the most amazing responses. They would say things like, "It starts with the heart. If you're not coming at it from the heart, you are doing everyone involved a disfavor," and "You have to be authentic when you are using influence; authenticity will help set you apart from others." Another powerful response was, "If you are trying to see possibilities in others, you can't help but influence for good."

Influence is a powerful force—it can build or destroy, heal or harm. Just like a river can nourish a valley or flood it, the way we use our influence matters. You've seen it in your own life: a kind word from a mentor that pushes you forward, or a harsh comment that lingers, holding you back. It's the same energy, directed in different ways.

On one hand, positive influence can uplift, inspire, and motivate people to achieve their best. It can foster growth, build confidence, and create a supportive and collaborative environment. For example, a teacher who encourages their students to believe in their potential can ignite a passion for learning that lasts a lifetime. Similarly, a leader who listens to their team's ideas and empowers them can boost morale and drive innovation.

On the other hand, influence can also be used negatively to manipulate, control, or deceive. Negative influence can undermine trust, create conflict, and lead to harmful behaviors or decisions. For instance, a leader who uses fear and intimidation to get results may achieve short-term success, but this approach can erode trust, stifle creativity, and cause long-term damage to team and organizational culture.

Your task as a GIVER is to harness your influence for the good of others. It's about understanding the weight your words and actions carry. By embracing the productive aspects of influence while being vigilant against its potential for harm, you can ensure that your influence contributes to the greater good.

Your Sphere of Influence

Recognize who influences you and whom you have the potential to influence. Influence isn't just about direct interactions; it includes subtle, indirect effects on those around you. Your sphere of influence encompasses family, friends, colleagues, and even acquaintances who observe and are impacted by your actions and decisions.

I remember the day I truly understood my sphere of influence. It was a typical Tuesday at the office, nothing special. I was grabbing a drink in the break room when a newer employee approached me. "I just wanted to thank you," she said. "I've been watching how you walk people through their questions and concerns to help them make a buying decision, and it's really helped me improve my own approach."

I was stunned. I hadn't directly interacted with her much, let alone tried to mentor her. Yet here she was, telling me

I'd influenced her work. It hit me then—my actions were having an impact far beyond what I realized.

This realization was both thrilling and terrifying. On one hand, I felt a sense of pride knowing I could positively influence others without even trying. On the other, I felt the weight of responsibility. If my actions were being observed and emulated, I needed to be more mindful of how I conducted myself.

As I reflected on this encounter, I started to see my influence everywhere. It was in the way my kids mimicked my mannerisms, how my friends sought my advice, and even in how the men I work with at church have started to show up differently to our meetings and activities. My sphere of influence, I realized, was like an invisible web connecting me to everyone around me.

I began to understand that this sphere had different layers. There was my inner circle: my family and closest friends. These were the people I interacted with most, the ones who saw me at my best and worst. Then there was my extended circle: colleagues, acquaintances, neighbors. While our interactions might be less frequent or deep, I was still leaving an impression on them.

But what really fascinated me was the potential circle— people I hadn't even met yet, but who might be influenced by my actions or words someday. It was like standing on the edge of a vast, unexplored territory of potential connections and impacts.

This understanding changed how I approached my daily life. Every interaction, no matter how small, became an opportunity to make a positive impact. I started to see myself not just as an individual, but as a node in a vast network of influence.

As we dive deeper into this concept, I want you to think about your own sphere of influence. Who are the people in your inner circle? Your extended circle? What about your potential circle? Understanding these layers is the first step in harnessing your influence to become a true GIVER.

Consider the different layers of your sphere of influence:

Inner Circle: These are your family and closest friends, the people with whom you have the most frequent and intimate interactions. Your influence on them is significant because of the strong emotional bonds and trust you've built over time.

Extended Circle: This includes colleagues, neighbors, and members of your community. Your interactions with them might be less frequent, but they still observe your behavior and can be influenced by your actions and words.

Potential Circle: These are individuals or groups you haven't yet connected with but who have the potential to influence through your actions, work, or presence in various settings. This could include social media followers, participants in community events, or people in professional networks.

Years ago, in a previous career, I was promoted to sales manager over a team of 12 sales reps. This promotion was the result of years of hard work, but I quickly realized that managing people was vastly different from simply doing the work myself. I knew I had to become a leader, not just a manager, and that meant learning new skills and approaches.

Seeking to become a better leader, I found a mentor in another manager named Derek. Derek's influence on me was subtle yet long lasting. He invested significant time in guiding me, not through direct orders but through thought-provoking questions that made me reflect deeply on my actions and decisions. He recommended books and articles on leadership, pointing out traits and behaviors in others that I should emulate or avoid.

One of the most impactful things Derek did was to point out the leadership qualities in those around us. For instance, during meetings, he would discreetly highlight how certain managers handled challenging situations with grace and empathy. He also wasn't shy about pointing out mistakes and suggesting how they could have been handled better. This approach helped me see leadership in action and understand the subtleties of effective influence.

Over time, I became more equipped to lead my team. I learned to listen actively, provide constructive feedback, and inspire my team to achieve their best. The skills Derek taught me didn't just help in my professional life; they spilled over into my personal life, helping me become a better husband, friend, and community member.

Derek's influence had a lasting constructive impact on my career and personal growth. His mentorship showed me that influence isn't always about direct control but often about guiding, supporting, and inspiring others through thoughtful actions and genuine concern for their development.

Building Trust: The Cornerstone of Influence

Trust is the cornerstone of influence. To build trust, you must establish genuine connections and demonstrate authenticity. People are more likely to be influenced by someone they trust and feel a genuine connection with.

> Trust is built over time through consistent, honest, and empathetic interactions.

Here are what I call the five Bs for building trust:

Be Genuine and Authentic: Engage with people sincerely. Ask about their lives, interests, and concerns. Listen actively and respond thoughtfully.

Be Consistent: Reliability is crucial. Follow through on your commitments and be consistent in your actions and words.

Be Transparent: Honesty is fundamental to building trust. Be open about your intentions, and communicate clearly and honestly.

Be Empathetic: Understand and respect others' feelings and perspectives. Showing empathy helps to create a strong emotional connection. (This is the third chapter in a row that discusses empathy. Watch for it and other key practices that appear in different chapters. They appear a lot for a reason.)

Be Respect: Treat everyone with respect, regardless of their status or background. Respect fosters mutual trust and cooperation.

About 10 years ago, I moved to a new neighborhood and started attending a different church. Shortly after, I was assigned to teach a Sunday school class for 15 to 16-year-olds. This was a group of wonderful young men and women, most of whom were enthusiastic about attending church and participating in the class. There was one young man who was an exception. He identified as an atheist and only attended because his father made him. Each week, he would sit at the back of the class, leaning against the wall, showing little interest in the discussions.

Determined to build a relationship with him, I realized I needed to change my approach. I started each class by asking everyone to share the best thing that happened to them that week. This small change began to create an atmosphere of sharing and mutual respect. As each student shared their stories, this young man would occasionally comment, showing brief glimpses of engagement.

When it was his turn, I made a special effort to show genuine interest in his stories. I asked follow-up questions about his hobbies and interests, delving deeper into the topics he cared about. Week by week, his responses grew longer, and he started to look forward to these interactions.

One Sunday, as the class was shuffling in, I immediately asked him a question about a hobby he was passionate about. He stopped in the middle of the room, engaged in the conversation, and for the first time, sat in the chair closest to me. This was a significant shift. By consistently showing interest and respect, I had built a bridge of trust.

Over the following weeks, he became more active in class discussions and started to enjoy attending. His transformation was remarkable, and he even began to contribute valuable insights during our lessons. A few years later, he made the surprising decision to serve a mission for our church. His father told me that my influence had played a significant role in his son's decision.

This experience reinforced the importance of trust and genuine connection. By being authentic, empathetic, and consistently showing interest in this young man's life, I was able to build a strong, trust-based relationship. This trust not only changed his attitude towards the class but also had a profound impact on his life choices.

In your journey to becoming a GIVER, remember that trust is not built overnight. It requires patience, consistency, and genuine care. But once established, trust becomes a powerful foundation for positive influence, enabling you to make a meaningful impact on those around you.

As we move forward, remember that trust is just the beginning. In the next chapter, we will explore how to leverage the trust you've built to create intentional and impactful influence. We'll review strategies for using your gifts and superpowers to inspire and lead others in a purposeful and meaningful way.

___

The Power of Listening

Active listening is a powerful tool for influence. By truly understanding the needs and perspectives of others, you build deeper connections that form the foundation of meaningful influence. Listening is more than just hearing words; it's about understanding the emotions, intentions, and contexts behind those words. When people feel heard and understood, they are more likely to trust and open up to you, allowing your influence to grow naturally.

Key Elements of Active Listening:

Full Attention: Give your undivided attention to the speaker, making them feel valued and respected.

Non-Verbal Cues: Use body language such as nodding, maintaining eye contact, and leaning forward to show engagement.

Reflective Listening: Paraphrase or summarize what the speaker has said to ensure understanding and show that you are listening. (Listening is another one of those key skills that will show up in many chapters.)

Open-Ended Questions: Ask questions that encourage the speaker to elaborate, providing deeper insights.

Empathy: Show empathy by acknowledging the speaker's feelings and perspectives.

Active listening was crucial in building trust with that young man at church. It gradually helped him open up and even look forward to attending. His very outlook transformed. I learned through this experience that being present and genuinely interested in the lives of others is the core of listening as a conscious practice. Applying Active Listening in Your Life

Let's explore how this plays out in different aspects of our lives. In each of these areas, active listening can be a game-changer, opening doors to deeper understanding and more meaningful connections:

Personal Relationships: Practice active listening with your family and friends. Show genuine interest in their lives, ask open-ended questions, and reflect on what they say. This strengthens your relationships and deepens your influence.

Professional Settings: Use active listening with colleagues and clients. Understand their needs, challenges, and aspirations. This builds trust and makes your influence more effective in driving collaborative efforts and achieving common goals.

Community Involvement: Engage with community members through active listening. Whether volunteering or participating in local events, understanding the community's needs and perspectives helps you contribute more meaningfully.

Ethical Influence

Ethical influence is about using your power or skills to help others in a fair and honest way, creating a positive impact that benefits everyone involved. It's the practice of guiding and inspiring others with integrity, transparency, and respect, ensuring that your actions align with your values and the greater good.

Principles of Ethical Influence:

Transparency and Honesty: Always be clear about your intentions and motivations. Avoid hidden agendas and ensure that your actions are guided by honesty and integrity.

Respect and Empathy: Treat others with respect and understanding. Consider their perspectives and needs, and aim to create mutually beneficial outcomes.

Accountability: Be responsible for your actions and their impact. If your influence leads to unintended consequences, take steps to address and rectify the situation.

Long-Term Impact: Focus on creating lasting positive change. Avoid quick fixes or short-term gains that could harm others in the long run.

At the tail end of the global pandemic in 2020, our office admin, Erin, was diagnosed with cancer. Her treatments required extended periods away from work, which could have significantly impacted our small business operations. We made a commitment to fully backing Erin in her battle, embodying our core value of being a "Force of Nature."

We made it possible for Erin to work from home when needed, kept her on payroll, and ensured her benefits remained active. Our team rallied together, covering her responsibilities to the best of our abilities. This decision, rooted in compassion and support, strengthened our team and had a lasting positive impact on Erin's life. By prioritizing her well-being over short-term business concerns, we demonstrated ethical influence in action. This experience reinforced the importance of making decisions that benefit everyone involved and maintaining integrity and empathy in our actions.

Ethical influence is a powerful tool for creating a positive impact in all areas of your life. By understanding and embracing the principles of ethical influence, you can ensure that your actions benefit everyone involved and contribute to a better world.

Exercises and Actionable Content

As you reflect on the lessons from this chapter, remember that influence is a powerful tool that can shape lives. Who's in your sphere? How can you show up for them in a way that lifts them up? How will you listen, build trust, and make sure your influence always comes from a place of integrity?

This chapter's worksheets contain tools for mapping your sphere of influence, identifying your natural communication style, and more.

You can access the Chapter 4 worksheet by going to www.thegivermethod.com/chapter-4-worksheets

---

Chapter 5:
Impactful vs. Intentional

Applying Your Gifts and Superpowers
With Purpose and Presence

"It takes tremendous discipline to control the influence, the power you have over other people's lives."
– Clint Eastwood

Sam, my wife's grandpa, had a unique way of raising his children, grandchildren, and great-grandchildren.

In Sam's kitchen, you couldn't just throw out statements you thought were true or say things for shock value without being able to back them up. If you made a claim, you had to understand and support what you were saying. For instance, if you commented on a political candidate by saying, "Oh man, that guy is stupid, or he doesn't know what he's doing," Sam would challenge you to explain why you felt that way. He wanted to know that your thoughts and opinions were backed by reason and evidence.

Sam's approach was rooted in integrity and a drive for truth. He had the courage to challenge others to think critically and study more deeply. This practice encouraged his children, grandchildren, and great-grandchildren to dive deeper into their thinking, studying, and to challenge other people's perspectives thoughtfully.

By consistently performing this simple yet intentional act, Sam created a massive impact on generations of individuals. His legacy is a testament to how intentional actions, grounded in a quest for truth and understanding, can lead to profound and lasting influence.

In this chapter, we will explore how to apply your influence with both impact and intentionality. You will learn to balance making a significant impact with being mindful of your intentions behind every action.

Making Your Influence Both Impactful and Intentional

Impactful and Intentional Influence within the GIVER Method

Sometimes, a simple word, gesture, or act of kindness can create a ripple effect you never anticipated. But other times, especially when the stakes are high, you need to step in with intention, carefully directing your influence toward a specific outcome. In this chapter, we're going to explore how to balance both types of influence—*impactful* and *intentional*—so that your influence always comes from a place of purpose.

Impactful Influence involves using your natural abilities to create significant changes in others' lives. This type of influence often happens organically and can have profound effects without requiring meticulous planning. It's about recognizing the potential your actions and words have to shape others' thoughts, behaviors, and attitudes. For instance, a spontaneous act of kindness or a casual conversation can leave a lasting impression on someone.

Intentional Influence, on the other hand, requires a deliberate approach. It means you are consciously directing your efforts to achieve a specific outcome. This involves strategic planning, goal setting, and a thoughtful understanding of how best to apply your gifts and superpowers in different situations. Intentional influence is about being present and aware of your actions, ensuring they align with your broader objectives and values.

Within the GIVER Method, balancing these two types of influence allows you to use your gifts and superpowers to their fullest potential. This balance is essential for disciplined influence.

A Personal Story

When reflecting on the balance between making a significant impact and being mindful of my intentions, I often think about how I apply the GIVER Method to help others tackle their complex problems. I frequently sit down with individuals to help them sift through their work, finances, and expenses, searching for opportunities they can leverage before seeking external assistance to cover their bills.

In the short term, my goal is to ensure there is food on their table and their bills are paid. While I'm here to provide support now, my long-term aim is to equip them with the skills and confidence they need to thrive on their own. My intention is to guide them towards this self-reliance.

During these financial reviews, I sometimes notice patterns of spending that could be improved—such as eating out frequently or subscribing to unnecessary apps and services. My immediate impulse might be to say, "Well, stop wasting your money," but I know that doing so would likely shut them down to my advice. This would hinder their ability to make the long-term changes I hope to see.

To balance impactful influence with intentionality, I focus on showing love, compassion, and understanding. Instead of being blunt, I approach these tough topics with empathy. By being intentional in my communication, I can guide them through the necessary changes without alienating them. This approach helps them create a realistic plan to achieve self-reliance.

Through this process, I've seen individuals gradually take control of their finances and work towards a more stable and independent future. The balance between impactful actions and mindful intentions has been crucial in fostering trust and facilitating meaningful, lasting change.

Differentiating Impactful vs. Intentional Influence

Understanding the difference between impactful and intentional influence is like learning to play a musical instrument. At first, you might create some pleasant sounds by chance—that's impactful influence. But as you practice and learn, you start to create beautiful music on purpose—that's intentional influence. Both are valuable, but they work in different ways.

I remember when I first grasped this concept. I was mentoring a newer member of my team at work who was very inexperienced in the position she had accepted, and I shared a personal story about overcoming self-doubt. Weeks later, she told me how that story had inspired her to move past self doubt she had been feeling as a part of taking this job. I hadn't planned for my story to have that effect, but it did. That was impactful influence.

On the flip side, there was a time when I carefully prepared a presentation to convince my team to adopt a new workflow. I considered their perspectives, anticipated objections, and crafted my message to address their concerns. When they agreed to give it a try, that was intentional influence at work.

Understanding these two types of influence is crucial for several reasons. First, it helps you recognize the full scope of your impact on others. You're not just influencing people when you're trying to—you're doing it all the time, often without realizing it. Second, it allows you to be more strategic in your interactions. When you understand both types of influence, you can choose the right approach for each situation.

Moreover, this understanding is key to using your influence ethically and effectively. Impactful influence often comes from your authentic actions and can create unexpected positive changes. Intentional influence, on the other hand, allows you to direct your efforts towards specific goals. As we dive deeper into each, I want you to think about times in your own life when you've experienced or used each type. Maybe you've inspired someone without meaning to, or perhaps you've carefully planned how to motivate your team. Both are powerful tools in your GIVER toolkit.

Impactful Influence

Impactful influence refers to the effects you have on others that often occur without a deliberate plan or conscious effort. This type of influence is more about the real-world outcomes and changes that result from your actions and words, often in unexpected ways.

Focus on the Actual Effect: Impactful influence is about the tangible effects your actions have on others, regardless of your intentions. It's the observed change in their thoughts, feelings, or behaviors.

Look at the Potential Outcomes and Observed Change: This type of influence is characterized by the noticeable changes it brings about in people. These changes can be positive or negative and are often recognized after the fact.

Characteristics:

- Unexpected Returns: The influence happens naturally, sometimes unexpectedly, and without premeditation.

- Observable Outcomes: There are tangible reactions or changes in others' behavior, attitudes, or beliefs as a result of your actions.

- Long-Lasting Effects: The influence tends to have a lasting impact, shaping perspectives or actions over time.

- Reflective: You often realize the impact of your influence upon reflection or through feedback from others.

Examples of Impactful Influence:

1. Changing the Direction of a Friend or Family Member's Life: Think of a time when your actions or words had a profound, lasting effect on someone close to you, even if it wasn't planned.

2. Impact Felt Over Time: Reflect on an instance where something you did or said had a ripple effect, influencing others far beyond the initial interaction.

3. Casual Compliment Inspiring Significant Change: You casually compliment a colleague on their work, and this simple act of recognition motivates them to pursue a new opportunity or project with renewed confidence.

4. Personal Story Motivating Someone Unexpectedly: You share a personal story during a casual conversation about overcoming a significant challenge. Unintentionally, this story inspires a

listener to tackle their own difficult project, and they later credit your story for their newfound motivation.

Intentional Influence

Intentional influence is a deliberate and strategic effort to guide or change someone's behavior, attitudes, or beliefs. This type of influence involves purposeful actions and thoughtful planning to achieve specific outcomes.

Focus and Conscious Effort: Intentional influence requires a conscious and proactive approach. It's about making a deliberate decision to influence a person or a group in a particular way.

Planning With a Specific Goal in Mind: This type of influence is goal-oriented. You set clear, specific objectives that you aim to achieve through your actions and strategies.

Characteristics:

- Deliberate Actions: Every step you take is carefully considered and aligned with your overall goal.

- Strategic Communication: You use precise and tailored communication techniques, such as persuasive arguments, emotional appeals, or data-driven presentations.

- Goal-Oriented: Your influence is directed towards achieving a particular result or change, making your efforts more focused and effective.

- Adaptive: You are flexible and adjust your approach based on the audience's needs, preferences, and responses, ensuring that your influence remains effective in varying situations.

Examples of Intentional Influence:

1. Helping Guide a Friend In Hard Times: Think of a time when you intentionally supported a friend through a difficult period. What steps did you take to be there for them, and how did you plan your actions to have the best impact?

2. Teaching Kids and Youth: Reflect on an experience where you intentionally taught or mentored young people. What were your goals, and how did you tailor your approach to meet their needs?

3. Giving a Persuasive Presentation: You prepare thoroughly, gather supporting data, anticipate potential objections, and craft your message to address concerns and highlight advantages, aiming to convince your audience to adopt a new software

tool.

4. Offering Specific Feedback to a Colleague: You provide detailed, constructive criticism aimed at improving their performance. You focus on specific areas for improvement and suggest actionable steps they can take.

For the last seven years, I have held various leadership roles within my church. I was responsible for the young men aged 12-18, served as the executive secretary for our bishop, and currently lead all the men in our congregation. In each of these roles, I've strived to use vulnerability to create impactful influence. Often, church leaders are perceived as "having it all together," making it difficult for some members to see themselves in our shoes. To bridge this gap, I use vulnerability to make a sincere connection.

I am the first to tell them, "I don't have all the answers," and "I struggle just as you do." What really resonates with people is when I share my struggle with wanting to attend church. Raised attending weekly services, I stopped going altogether at the age of 22. I became completely inactive in church activities, and my testimony was weak. During this time, I faced numerous struggles: I was unhappy with my employment, faced financial difficulties, experienced mental health challenges, and struggled in my relationship with my wife.

I can relate to those who hurt, feel lost, depressed, or unheard. When I open up and share my vulnerabilities, I create a deeper connection and offer hope and someone they can turn to. Yes, if you see me on Sunday, I may be in a three-piece suit, sitting with my happy family, appearing as though I've had it all together my entire life. But the truth of where I've been and how I got to where I am today is what continues to draw people in.

Application in Daily Life

To differentiate between the two, consider the following aspects:

Awareness and Intention: Reflect on whether your influence in a situation was planned or happened organically. Did you set out with a specific goal to influence others, or did it occur as a byproduct of your actions?

Feedback and Reflection: Pay attention to feedback from others and your own reflections. If people often tell you that something you said or did inspired or changed them, you might be having impactful influence. If you consistently work towards influencing outcomes, you're practicing intentional influence.

Outcome Analysis: Look at the outcomes of your interactions. Intentional influence tends to produce predictable, goal-aligned results, while impactful influence may have broader, sometimes unexpected effects.

Methodology: Consider your methods. Are you using structured approaches like persuasive presentations, motivational techniques, or strategic planning? This indicates intentional influence. If your influence comes from being a role model or sharing your experiences naturally, it's more likely impactful.

By understanding and recognizing these differences, you can better tap into both types of influence to create positive changes in your personal and professional life.

Additional Points to Consider:

- Intention doesn't guarantee impact. You can have the best intentions, but your influence may not have the desired effect.

- Impact can be delayed. Someone you influence today may not react until later, making it hard to link cause and effect.

- Impact can be subtle. A small change in someone's behavior can be a significant outcome.

Tips to be a more impactful influencer:

- Consider your audience: Tailor your communication style and approach to the person you're trying to influence.

- Focus on building relationships: Trust and rapport make people more receptive to your influence.

- Be clear and concise: Communicate your message effectively to avoid misunderstandings.

- Be mindful of nonverbal cues: Body language and tone of voice can significantly impact how your message is received.

- Be open to feedback: Be receptive to how your influence is perceived and adjust your approach if needed.

Balancing Impact and Intention

To tap into both types of influence effectively:

- Be Mindful: Recognize that your actions and words can have both intended and unintended effects. Strive to be mindful of the potential impacts you can have.

- Reflect and Learn: Regularly reflect on your interactions and the outcomes they produce. Learn from both your planned efforts and the unexpected influences you observe.

- Adapt and Evolve: Be open to adapting your strategies based on feedback and new insights. This continuous learning approach helps you refine your influence to be both impactful and intentional.

Balancing intentional and impactful influence is especially relevant in long-term relationships. My wife and I have a rule that we won't end the day angry with each other. We've set this intention with the understanding of both the short-term and long-term impacts it will have on our relationship.

This practice hasn't always been easy. We've had some long, tough nights working through disagreements. In the heat of an argument, it's tempting to say things just to prove a point. But we've learned that these words don't reflect our true feelings and can damage the relationship in the long run. By focusing on the longer-term outcomes, we aim to resolve conflicts by the end of the day.

This intention helps us wake up with a clean slate, which positively affects how we interact with each other, how we parent our boys, and how we engage with the world. Being both intentional and impactful in our approach ensures that our relationship remains strong and harmonious.

This balance has taught me that being intentional in resolving conflicts leads to impactful, positive outcomes. It reinforces the importance of addressing issues with care and understanding, fostering a deeper connection and a healthier relationship.

The Long-Term Impact of Intentional Influence

When you influence with the long-term in mind, you are planting seeds that will grow and flourish, sometimes in ways you might not immediately see. I reflect on how my wife and I are raising our three boys. We want them not only to do chores but also to keep a tidy house and, eventually, lead healthy, happy lives. Since they were little, we've involved them in cleaning tasks based on their abilities.

For example, we started with our two-year-old by having him pick up toys and throw away trash. As our other boys got a little older, they began clearing their dinner plates. As they grew, we introduced more complex chores like unloading and loading the dishwasher, doing laundry, and cleaning their rooms.

We don't pay an allowance for these chores. We've taught them that keeping a house clean is a family responsibility, and we all have to work together to maintain it. We discuss why cleanliness is important, emphasizing how it helps keep our bodies healthy, our minds focused, and our environment organized. We point out how they feel when their surroundings are clean and organized.

As our boys have grown, I've seen our teachings take effect. Our oldest, who is now 14, often does chores without being asked and picks up after himself without constant reminders. While they're still young boys who can be messy, they are doing better at maintaining cleanliness than I did at their age.

This progress started with our intentional efforts as parents to influence our children's growth. We already see the long-term impact of our approach and can envision its continued benefits as they grow older.

Being a Gift GIVER to Those You Influence

As we near the end of this chapter, I want you to take a moment and really let everything sink in. Think about how far you've come on this journey. Remember when we first talked about discovering your gifts? It might have seemed daunting at first, but look at you now—you've not only identified your unique talents but you've also mapped out your sphere of influence. And now, you're learning the delicate dance of balancing impact and intention.

I recall when I first started putting all these pieces together. It was like solving a complex puzzle, and suddenly, the picture became clear. I realized that being a true GIVER wasn't just about random acts of kindness; it was about strategically using my gifts to make a real difference in people's lives.

Over 12 years ago, I was working for an amazing company with a culture I wanted to be a part of, especially after experiencing numerous negative working environments. Unexpectedly, I was let go. Shocked and scrambling to find a job, I ended up in a large company with a toxic culture.

I kept my head down and worked, but I eventually heard about a company with a reputation for having an amazing culture and core values that aligned with my own. I applied and started the interview process. I thought I was doing well, but after one of the interview rounds, Brad, the owner of the company, called to inform me they were not moving me forward. Even though he was not going to hire me he gave me this amazing advice: "Whether you use this in the future to work here or somewhere else, here are some things you can do that will change how you show up." One piece of advice stood out: "When you interview or do anything, give it 100% of your effort and attention. Most people never put 100% into what they are doing, so you will immediately stand out."

I took his advice to heart, particularly the part about giving 100%. The next year, when the same company was hiring again, I applied. This time, I approached the process differently. I gave 100% to every step they asked of me. Punchline of the story, I beat out all other candidates because of how prepared I was for my final interview. Brad's advice changed and elevated my approach, and I secured the job.

The lessons Brad taught me have become integral to how I live daily. As new opportunities arise, I have a robust toolkit to draw from to be intentional and make an impact. This transformation was due to Brad's intentional influence and the impact he aimed to make through his hiring process and the advice he gave when he turned me down. I will forever be grateful for the massive change this has had on my life and where I am headed.Now, it's your turn to put this into practice. Think about the people in your life - your family, friends, colleagues, community members. How can you be a Gift GIVER to them? How can you intentionally use your unique talents to uplift and support them? And how might your actions create unexpected positive impacts?

Remember, being a Gift GIVER isn't about grand gestures or life-altering events. It's about consistently showing up, using your gifts, and being mindful of both your intentions and your impact. It's about being authentic and generous with your talents, knowing that your influence can create positive change, whether you plan it or not.

Exercises and Actionable Content

This chapter's worksheets contain methods for impactful action plans, long-term goal setting, intentionality auditing, and more.

You can access the Chapter 5 worksheet by going to www.thegivermethod.com/chapter-5-worksheets

- Regular Revisions: Make it a habit to review and update your worksheets frequently. This will help you stay aligned with your goals and adapt to new insights and feedback.

- Reflect and Adjust: Use the insights gained from your intentionality audits and reflections to make necessary adjustments to your action plans.

- Stay Committed: Remember that the journey to becoming a GIVER is ongoing. Embrace the process of continuous learning and improvement.

Chapter 6:
Value

Creating and Delivering Meaningful Value

"If we can fall in love with serving people, creating value, solving problems, building valuable connections, and doing work that matters, it makes it far more likely we're going to do important work." - Seth Godin

---

Now, you've begun to recognize your potential to leave a lasting impact. But as we move forward, it's time to ask ourselves—what comes next?

To me, concepts like defining your purpose, moving beyond recognition, and building trust and credibility are often overlooked when people try to give value using their gifts and superpowers. In a business community I am part of, one of my clients runs a group program for small business owners, and we had discussed it extensively. The members of this group fit my ideal client profile perfectly— they were the right size of business and operated in areas where we could make a significant impact.

One day, I asked my client if I could start joining their weekly calls. I wanted to ensure he didn't think I was doing this to find potential clients. I told him, "I will attend the calls every week, support what you are coaching them on, and deliver as much value to them as I can, but I will never make a pitch or ask them to work with me. I want to share what I have with them and see them improve." I was giving without expecting anything in return, moving beyond the need for recognition.

Over time, I became a valuable resource for the members of his program. Not surprisingly, because I was offering so much value, many of the members reached out to me directly, asking how we could work together one-on-one to impact their business. In fact, this group has become one of our best sources of clients, and not once have I made a pitch or even hinted at someone working with us. I just showed up, delivered my gift to them, and the universe found a way to pay me back.

That's where the "V" in GIVER comes in—*Value*. This chapter is all about creating and delivering meaningful value using our gifts and superpowers. Remember, influence is at its best when it delivers the most value possible. We will explore how to move from merely recognizing our strengths to actively applying them to make a tangible difference in the lives of those we influence. Delivering value using your gifts and superpowers is one of the most important parts of the GIVER Method. Even more important is delivering that value without asking for anything in return. We live in a world filled with people who will scratch your back if you scratch theirs. Often, the value being exchanged isn't equal. Instead, it's better to approach giving from the perspective of offering without expecting anything in return.

Through this chapter, we will dive deeper into this idea and explore how your unique gifts and superpowers can bring value to those in your sphere of influence. By focusing on selfless giving, you can create a more meaningful and impactful presence in the lives of others.

Acknowledging Struggles

Of course, translating your unique gifts and superpowers into tangible value for others can be incredibly rewarding, but it's not without its challenges. Let's talk about some common hurdles you might face and how to overcome them.

One of the first challenges is a lack of self-awareness. Sometimes, we don't fully understand our own gifts and superpowers. It's like having a treasure chest but not knowing what's inside. To tackle this, spend some time reflecting on your strengths. Ask yourself what you're naturally good at and enjoy doing. And don't hesitate to seek feedback from friends and family—they often see things in us that we overlook.

Another hurdle is difficulty communicating value. It's one thing to know you have a gift or superpower, but explaining how it benefits others can be tricky. To overcome this, develop a clear message about your gifts and superpowers. Think about times when you've made a positive impact and use those stories to illustrate your point. Storytelling is a powerful tool to help others understand the value you bring.

Identifying compatibility is also crucial. Not everyone will be receptive to your gifts and superpowers, and that's okay. Focus on those who have expressed a need or interest that aligns with what you have to offer. It's like finding the right audience for your message—you want to connect with people who will truly benefit from your abilities.

Then there's the challenge of finding the right application. Even if you know your gift or superpower and have people who value it, figuring out the best way to use it can be daunting. Active listening is just as important here. Engage with the people you want to help, understand their challenges, and tailor your approach to fit their specific needs. It's about being flexible and responsive to ensure your efforts are effective.

Misalignment with others' needs can also be a barrier. Sometimes, your gifts and superpowers may not directly align with what others need at the moment. To bridge this gap, take time to understand their needs fully and adapt your application accordingly. It's about being empathetic and willing to adjust your approach to meet them where they are.

One of my superpowers is the ability to break down complex processes and simplify them so they can be implemented into software. This is something I've done for years, helping countless small businesses save time, energy, and money, ultimately increasing their profitability. In my field, I'm known as an expert for this skill. As I interact with people I know outside of work who own small businesses and face issues I could help with, my offers of ideas and suggestions are often met with resistance and skepticism.

Since they aren't fully aware of what I do, and they might not be ready to hear what I have to say, they often shut down my ideas. This happened for years—me trying to give them my gift and them turning it down again and again. Over time, I came to a couple of realizations. First, some businesses just aren't ready for what I can offer. Second, there's a way I can present the value I have without getting shut down.

Now, when I hear about their struggles, I start by saying, "I had a client experiencing something similar to this. In fact, what we did had these types of results for them. Would you like to talk through some of this and see if there's something I can offer to help?" More and more people have become open to the value I can provide.

As we continue on the path learning about Value, we'll dive deeper into how to navigate resistance and effectively communicate the value of your gifts and superpowers. By learning from these experiences, we can better understand how to approach others and offer our help in ways that are both impactful and well-received.

Understanding Value

Creating value goes beyond transactional exchanges. It's about recognizing the intrinsic worth of principles and qualities and serving others selflessly. When we focus on creating meaningful value, we consider both tangible and intangible aspects of our influence. Here's a deeper look at how value can be both tangible and intangible:

When I first started thinking about value, I imagined it in terms of concrete, measurable things—like helping a friend move or teaching someone a new skill. These tangible forms of value are easy to recognize and appreciate. They're the kind of help you can see, touch, or immediately put to use. But as I grew in my understanding of what it means to be a GIVER, I realized there's a whole other dimension to value that's just as important, if not more so.

This intangible value is harder to measure, but its impact can be profound. It's the encouragement that boosts someone's confidence, the empathy that makes someone feel understood, or the inspiration that motivates someone to pursue their dreams. I remember a time when a simple "I believe in you" from a mentor changed the entire trajectory of my career. That's the power of intangible value—it can transform lives in ways we might not even realize at the time.

As we explore the different forms of value you can offer as a GIVER, keep in mind this interplay between tangible and intangible.

> Your skills and expertise might provide tangible value, while your personal qualities often create intangible value.

The impact and outcomes of your actions can span both realms. By recognizing and intentionally cultivating both types of value, you'll be able to make a more holistic and lasting difference in the lives of others.

Here are some of the tangible and intangible ways you can create value:

Skills and Expertise

Problem-Solving Abilities: Your ability to tackle challenges and find solutions can significantly improve someone's situation. Whether it's helping a friend navigate a personal issue or advising a colleague on a project, your problem-solving skills can create immense value.

Knowledge and Experience: When you share your knowledge and experience, you create a cascade of learning and progress. This might involve mentoring someone in your field, offering advice based on your experiences, or teaching a skill you've mastered.

Technical Skills: Your technical abilities, whether they are in coding, design, or another area, can be a tremendous asset. Helping someone build a website, fix a technical issue, or improve their digital skills are examples of how technical expertise creates value.

Personal Qualities

Trustworthiness: Being reliable and honest establishes a foundation of trust. When people know they can count on you, it fosters stronger relationships and a sense of security.

Empathy and Compassion: Showing understanding and care for others' feelings and situations can deeply impact their emotional well-being. Offering a listening ear or a shoulder to cry on can provide immense comfort.

Motivation and Work Ethic: Demonstrating dedication and a strong work ethic can inspire others to push themselves and achieve their goals. Your example can motivate and uplift those around you.

Communication Skills: Effective communication fosters clarity and mutual understanding. Whether it's resolving conflicts, providing feedback, or simply being a good conversationalist, your ability to communicate well can enhance relationships and productivity.

Impact and Outcomes

Past Performance: Reflecting on how you've successfully helped others in the past can guide your future actions. Your track record of delivering positive results builds credibility and trust.

Potential for Change: Your influence can catalyze significant changes in others' lives. Whether it's helping someone adopt a healthier lifestyle or encouraging them to pursue their dreams, the potential impact of your actions can be profound.

Contribution to Well-Being: Your actions can directly enhance someone's emotional, mental, or physical well-being. This could be through acts of kindness, providing support during tough times, or helping them develop healthier habits.

Intangible Value

Inspiration and Motivation: Your presence and actions can inspire others to become better versions of themselves. By living authentically and pursuing your passions, you encourage others to do the same.

Sense of Belonging and Community: Building a sense of belonging and community is essential. Whether through fostering inclusivity, organizing social gatherings, or simply being there for others, you can create an environment where people feel connected and supported.

Positive Influence on Perspective: Offering new ideas or challenging someone's thinking in a positive way can broaden their horizons and encourage growth. Your unique perspective can help others see situations differently and consider new possibilities.

Intrinsic Worth and Principles

Service Without Expectation: Serving others selflessly, without expecting anything in return, is a powerful way to create value. This could be through volunteering, helping a friend in need, or offering your time and skills to a cause you care about.

Integrity and Ethics: Acting with integrity and adhering to strong moral principles sets a powerful example. Your commitment to doing what's right, even when it's difficult, inspires others and builds trust.

Commitment to Principles: Staying true to your values and principles, especially in challenging situations, demonstrates strength of character. Your dedication to your beliefs can influence and encourage others to uphold their own values.

There are times when you don't fully grasp the value you've created for someone, especially when it feels like you've just done what you were supposed to. In case you missed it, there was a global pandemic in 2020 that essentially shut the world down. As the world slowly began to reopen and we were able to return to church, some individuals were encouraged not to return as quickly as others. Mainly for health concerns, it was advised that older individuals and those with health issues should take caution when returning to church. Knowing that our congregation would be split in this way, we began to think of ways to get the message to those at home.

Given that I work in technology and spend hours every day on Zoom, I was able to step in and explain how we could stream the services to those who had to stay home. I know this seems simple now because everyone is familiar with Zoom, but at that point, many were not. My church hadn't ever really provided Sunday services via zoom or any livestream process. You had to show up each week to her the messages being shared. I knew it was time for me to step in and provide some value for those who could not attend. I had some extra webcams and microphones around the house that I could use to get the speaker on camera and stream the service into people's homes.

One night, I stopped by the home of a member named Juanita, who was unable to return to church yet. She mentioned that she loved the streaming service but missed seeing everyone and hearing the music, as the microphone didn't pick up the music well. That week, I dug up another camera and ordered a microphone on Amazon that could pick up more sounds, like music. The following week, I set up a camera for the speaker and a separate camera facing the congregation, along with a mic to capture the music.

I found this all to be simple to do. Still to this day, members of our congregation continue to thank me and tell me how much of an impact it had on them. They appreciated not only being able to watch church from home but also feeling like they were there by seeing people's faces. When Juanita was finally able to return to church, she held my hand and expressed her deepest gratitude for bringing more joy into her home with this simple act.

So, remember that even if using a gift or superpower of yours seems simple, it can still have a major impact on someone's life that you may not even realize. Creating value is about more than just what you can give materially.

By focusing on both tangible and intangible aspects, you can ensure that your influence is not only impactful but also deeply meaningful.

Applying Gifts and Superpowers

So far, you've reflected on your strengths, skills, and unique qualities as well as defined your gifts and superpowers. Next, if you haven't done so already, define your purpose. You need to determine why you want to use your gifts and superpowers. You may have already done this as a part of previous chapters, but if you haven't, now is the time. Whether it's to inspire, support, teach, or innovate, having a clear purpose will guide your actions and keep you focused.

Moving beyond recognition to action is where the real value lies. Don't wait to be explicitly asked for help. Previous chapter exercises worked on how to proactively seek opportunities to utilize your gifts and superpowers, even if it means stepping outside your comfort zone. Engage with others to understand their needs and how your abilities can help.

Empowering others should be a primary focus. The ultimate goal isn't dependence, but empowerment. You know, the whole "teach a man to fish" idea. Use your gifts and superpowers to equip others with the tools and skills to navigate their own challenges. This creates a domino effect of positive change, extending the impact of your efforts.

Identifying Value Gaps

Value gaps represent those areas where the needs of others aren't fully met, and they offer you the perfect opportunity to step in and make a real difference. Here's how to identify and address these gaps effectively.

Understand Needs and Challenges

The first step in identifying value gaps is to immerse yourself in the world of the people you want to help. Spend time observing their daily lives, listening to their stories, and engaging in meaningful conversations. This isn't just about casual chats; it's about delving deep to gain a genuine understanding of their struggles and aspirations. By being present and attentive, you can uncover the nuanced needs that aren't immediately obvious.

Imagine talking to a colleague who seems overwhelmed with their workload. Through your conversations, you might discover that they're struggling with time management. This insight comes from truly listening and showing empathy, which opens the door to identifying a gap where you can offer support.

Identify Gaps in Solutions

Once you have a clear understanding of the needs and challenges, the next step is to evaluate the current solutions in place. Look at what's already being done to address these issues. Are the existing solutions effective? Where do they fall short? By critically analyzing these solutions, you can pinpoint areas of frustration and inefficiency.

Think about a community project where efforts to clean up a local park have stalled. Despite volunteers' best intentions, the park remains neglected. By examining what's been tried before and why it didn't work, you can identify specific shortcomings that need addressing.

Match Your Skills

Now that you've identified where the existing solutions fall short, reflect on your own skills and abilities. How can you use your unique talents to bridge these gaps? This step requires a bit of creativity. Think about how your strengths align with the needs you've identified and consider innovative ways to apply them.

If you have strong organizational skills, perhaps you could coordinate a more efficient schedule for the park cleanup, ensuring that volunteers are better utilized and that the effort is more sustained.

Create Unique Solutions

Developing unique solutions involves thinking outside the box. It's about using your creativity to come up with approaches that others might have overlooked. This is where your gifts and superpowers truly shine. By applying your skills in new and innovative ways, you can create solutions that are not only effective but also sustainable.

For example, instead of just organizing another cleanup day, you might set up a community engagement program that includes educational workshops about the importance of maintaining public spaces. This approach addresses the immediate need for a cleaner park while also fostering a sense of ownership and responsibility within the community.

By actively seeking out value gaps and creatively applying your strengths to fill them, you not only make a significant impact but also inspire others to see the potential for positive change. This approach ensures that your influence is both purposeful and deeply felt.

Sustainable Giving

Sustainable giving is about finding ways to offer consistent and impactful aid without burning yourself out. It's a balancing act that ensures you can keep giving over the long haul while maintaining your own well-being. Here's how to practice sustainable giving effectively:

Balance and Self-Care

The foundation of sustainable giving is taking care of yourself. This means prioritizing your physical, emotional, and mental health. Think of it like putting on your oxygen mask first in an airplane before helping others. If you're not well, your ability to help others diminishes. So, make sure you're getting enough rest, eating well, exercising, and taking time for activities that rejuvenate you.

Imagine a time when you felt particularly drained and had to take a step back to recharge. By prioritizing self-care, you can return to your efforts with renewed energy and a clearer mind.

Set Boundaries

Setting clear boundaries is crucial. Define when and how you're available to help others. This means being honest about your limits and not overcommitting yourself. It's okay to say no when you need to. Setting boundaries ensures that you have the time and energy to give effectively without feeling overwhelmed.

Consider a scenario where you were bombarded with requests for help and had to learn to say no to maintain your sanity. By setting boundaries, you create a sustainable rhythm for giving.

Focus on High-Impact Areas

Not all efforts yield the same results. Identify areas where your help can make the most significant difference and focus your energy there. This means being strategic about where you invest your time and resources, ensuring that your efforts have the maximum positive impact.

Think about a time when you identified a specific need that aligned perfectly with your skills and passions. By focusing on this high-impact area, you were able to create substantial and lasting change.

Collaborate with Others

You don't have to do it all alone. Partnering with others can multiply the impact of your efforts and reduce individual strain. Collaboration brings together diverse skills and perspectives, making your collective efforts more powerful and effective.

Recall a situation where teaming up with others made a project more successful than it would have been if you had tackled it alone. Collaboration not only eases the burden but also fosters a sense of community and shared purpose.

Seek Feedback and Adapt

Regularly ask for feedback from those you're helping and be open to making changes based on what you learn. This helps you stay effective and ensures that your efforts are truly meeting the needs of others. Adaptation is important to sustainability; it allows you to refine your approach and stay responsive to changing circumstances. Reflect on a time when you received constructive feedback that helped you improve your approach to giving..

Celebrate and Reflect

Acknowledging small wins along the way is important for maintaining motivation and morale. Take time to reflect on your journey, celebrate the progress you've made, and appreciate the impact you've had. This reflection helps you stay connected to your purpose and keeps you inspired to continue giving.

Think about a moment when you took a step back to celebrate a success, no matter how small. This celebration not only boosted your spirits but also reinforced your commitment to sustainable giving.

Think about a time when you didn't set clear boundaries while delivering value to others. As a natural GIVER, it can be hard to dial back. It can also lead to people becoming overly reliant on you, which often results in negative emotions. I've experienced this many times myself. Each time it happens, I find myself frustrated with the person seeking the value I can provide. Delivering value should bring joy, but without setting boundaries, it can have a negative impact. I want you to avoid the burnout that can come from this.

By integrating these principles into your giving practices, you ensure that your efforts are not only impactful but also sustainable. This approach allows you to keep making a worthwhile difference over the long term, benefiting both you and those you aim to help.

Daily Value Diary

Purpose: To track daily acts of giving value and reflect on their impact.

Instructions:

- Document Daily Acts: Each day, write down the acts of giving value you performed, the reactions from others, and how it made you feel.

- Weekly Reflection: Summarize your entries at the end of each week and reflect on the overall impact of your actions.

Tips:

- Be Consistent: Make it a daily habit to note your acts of giving, even if they seem small.

- Reflect Deeply: Consider not just what you did, but how it affected you and others emotionally and practically.

Exercises and Actionable Content

This chapter's worksheets offer exercises designed to help you identify and build the value you can offer using your gifts and superpowers. A generosity plan, value proposition, daily value diary, and more will help you foster a connection to your purpose.

You can access the Chapter 6 worksheet by going to www.thegivermethod.com/chapter-6-worksheets

Chapter 7:
How Value Becomes Vivid

Creating Vivid Value With Your
Gifts And Superpowers

"The secret to success is... no secret. It's called work your ass off and find a way to add more value to people's lives than anyone else does!" - Tony Robbins

---

By refining how we present our value, we can create experiences that are powerful, clear, and deeply appreciated. We will dive into the elements that make value vivid, such as personalization, storytelling, and visual impact, and learn how to apply these to our unique gifts and superpowers.

Personally, until I fully understood my gifts and superpowers and worked on developing them, I faced many difficulties. I often felt lost in my day-to-day life, primarily due to a lack of goals and self-awareness. I love the quote by Robert Heinlein: "In the absence of clearly defined goals, we become strangely loyal to daily trivia, until ultimately we become enslaved by it." Not knowing what I had to offer and not having clearly defined goals left me adrift in life, seriously impacting my mental health, relationships, and many other aspects of my life.

Becoming a true GIVER means mastering the art of creating vivid value. Let's break that down: *Vivid* means something that creates a strong image or feeling. It's bright, intense, impossible to ignore. *Value* is about what's useful and important. So when we talk about providing vivid value, we mean offering something so clear, so impactful, that it leaves a deep impression on the person receiving it.

Here's a quote I love to set the tone: "When you live your life in alignment with a purpose that is centered on selflessly adding value for others, opportunities become abundant and your life becomes fulfilled." - Hal Elrod

---

Providing Vivid Value: Leveraging Your Gifts and Superpowers for Lasting Impact

Imagine you have a superpower that allows you to access vast amounts of information and tailor learning experiences. Picture a student struggling with a complex historical concept. By creating an interactive simulation that places the student in the historical event, you allow them to make choices and experience the consequences. This personalized and engaging learning experience creates a deeper understanding and ignites a passion for history.

Over time, this approach could revolutionize education by catering to individual learning styles and fostering a love for lifelong learning.

Or consider if your superpower lies in mentorship and coaching. By offering ongoing mentorship to young professionals in your field, you can share your knowledge and experience through regular one-on-one sessions, workshops, and networking events. Your mentees gain valuable skills, confidence, and professional connections that help them advance their careers. The ripple effect occurs when they pass on the knowledge and mentorship they received to others.

I see this through the daily work I am doing with my team and with the clients we serve. A gift that I am working on to develop into a full superpower is a leadership skill that forces you to think about how you show up to those around you.

> We all have days when we show up as our best or as the A Player version of ourselves. We also all have plenty of slacker days or B Player versions of ourselves. The difference between the two is intention.

Now I practice this with my team all the time without them realizing I am doing it (oops, I guess the cat is out of the bag on this one). I find the little points to help them see that even in just the way they say a phrase, write an email, or make a statement about someone can have massive impacts on how they show up. I want them to develop intentionality as a gift of their own.

The same is true for our clients. They don't hire us to help them become better leaders, but we are constantly trying to rewire their thinking in how they show up. We drop little statements to them, we offer advice on how to handle situations, and anywhere else we can find the opening, we add it. I can't tell you how many clients, after months of working with us, finally realize how much they've changed in the time they have worked with us.

The ripple effect is this: I learned these skills from my mentors and have begun using them, and that is the first ripple. I then use those skills with my team, our clients, my family, and all those I connect with, creating a whole new set of ripples. When my team shows up differently to each other, their clients, friends, and family, that ripple is then passed off and continues through all of those connections. It then changes how our clients show up as leaders to their teams, their families, and friends, and so on.

I love the fact that I will never know how far my ripple has reached by working on how I deliver value to those I am in contact with daily and how that changes them over time as well.

Maybe you have the ability to translate languages and understand different cultural nuances. Imagine creating real-time translation devices that not only translate words but also capture cultural context and emotions. This innovation eliminates communication barriers and fosters deeper connections between people from diverse backgrounds. By bridging language barriers, you can foster a more inclusive and interconnected world, enhancing global collaboration.

Strong organizational skills and a passion for community service can lead to organizing regular community events, such as clean-ups, workshops, or social gatherings, that address local needs and foster a sense of community. These events help build a stronger, more connected community, encouraging ongoing participation and collaboration, and improving local quality of life.

If you have the ability to understand and respond to various communication styles and disabilities, you could create customized interfaces for individuals with disabilities. Offering text-to-speech, voice recognition, or alternative control methods ensures that everyone can access information and participate in the digital world. Revolutionizing accessibility creates a more inclusive digital landscape where everyone can thrive.

Consider your ability to process information and provide emotional support. Developing personalized mental health chatbots that offer emotional support, access to resources, and crisis intervention tools, all while respecting privacy and confidentiality, could significantly impact mental well-being and resilience. This is especially crucial in areas where traditional services are limited.

Finally, if you can analyze vast amounts of data and identify patterns, you could analyze scientific research papers and identify potential breakthroughs or undiscovered connections. This could accelerate scientific progress in various fields, contributing to solving global challenges like climate change and disease.

Unexpected Delight and Personal Touch

Creating Vivid Value isn't just about offering help; it's about exceeding expectations and leaving a recipient feeling truly delighted. Here's how unexpected delight and a personal touch can elevate your acts of giving from ordinary to unforgettable.

Think about the last time you went the extra mile for someone. Imagine you're helping a friend with a presentation. Instead of just creating a slide deck, you surprise them by researching and crafting compelling visuals or finding relevant quotes to add impact. This unexpected effort not only enhances the presentation but also shows your friend how much you care about their success.

Let me share an example that highlights the immense impact of a personal touch. Over the past few years, I've developed a close relationship with someone named Nima from a mastermind group. Nima is an amazing individual who has found his calling in the world of relationships. I've tried expressing to Nima how much his small gestures have impacted me, but I don't think he fully understands.

In previous chapters, I have mentioned that over the last few years, my brain has discovered the emotion of anxiety. Many times when it hits, it can shut me down completely for minutes, hours, or even the rest of the day. One day, I was having one of these anxiety attacks. I was thinking things like, "Why am I even trying?" "No one cares about what I am trying to do," and "I just can't do it all." I thought, "No one will ever care about this book or the GIVER Method; you are just wasting your time." I wanted to just walk out the door, go home, and go to bed. I lay down in my office, put on some music, and tried to clear my head when I received a Facebook message from Nima. It was a voice-recorded message.

In it, he said, "Hey brother, I just wanted you to know I was thinking about you and wanted to tell you how much I admire you and what you are doing. The way you show up and how you are trying to help everyone is inspiring to me. So I wanted to say thank you and hope everything is going well in your world." I listened to this and broke down into tears. His message touched me deeply and was so timely. Within a minute, my mind cleared, and I was able to go back to work. This small and simple personal gesture had a huge impact on me.

Since then, Nima and I send messages to each other at random, each replying with something like, "Man, I really needed to hear that today." I have made it my goal to never miss out on small prompts to stop and send an encouraging message, just like Nima did for me. He created so much value for me, and in turn, I get to pass that along to others.

Anticipating needs is another powerful way to create vivid value. Picture yourself mentoring a student who is struggling with test anxiety. By thinking ahead, you bring them a small stress ball or teach them relaxation techniques to manage their nerves. This thoughtful gesture addresses an unspoken need and can make a significant difference in their performance and well-being.

Sometimes, tiny acts of joy can create the biggest smiles. Offering a cup of coffee before starting a task, bringing a single flower "just because," or leaving a handwritten note expressing gratitude are small but powerful ways to show you care. These little surprises can brighten someone's day and strengthen your connection with them.

Storytelling and Visual Impact

Storytelling and visual elements are powerful tools to achieve vivid value. When you engage emotions and imagination, you make your advice more relatable. For instance, if you're mentoring someone, share a story about a time when you faced a similar challenge and how you overcame it. This approach not only makes your guidance more accessible but also shows that you understand their situation.

I try to use storytelling when I am delivering value and want to make a deeper connection with those I am engaging with. The best example I can give is the stories that I've put into this book. Once I knew what the GIVER Method was and that I needed to write this book, I spent months researching. I read every article and book I could find about Giving, Influence, Value, Engagement, and Relationships. I took vigorous notes, outlined the chapters, and filled the outline with every thought I had from my research. I then built out the worksheets to know what I am driving the reader towards. Finally, it came time to write out each chapter. I focused on packing them with valuable insights.

When I had my wife read through my initial drafts, she said, "You've got tons of amazing insights here, but this feels more like an academic paper and not a book where you are talking to the reader. You need to talk to the reader; you need to tell stories that can paint the picture you are trying to help them with, and you need to make it relatable." Once I started inserting stories into the chapters and letting others read through them, the feedback was overwhelmingly positive. I heard things like, "I love how personal it is." Everyone has stories to tell, and you are capable of the same.

Simplifying complex ideas is another way storytelling can be powerful. Suppose you're explaining a complicated business strategy. You could frame it as a story of a company navigating a journey, facing obstacles, and ultimately succeeding. This narrative helps your audience visualize the process and grasp the key points more easily, making the information more digestible and memorable.

Inspiring and motivating others can be effectively achieved through storytelling. Share a success story of someone who applied your advice or followed a similar path and achieved great results. This can inspire your audience to believe in their potential and take proactive steps, showing them that success is attainable.

Visual aids also play a crucial role in making your value offering vivid. If you're presenting a project plan, use a flowchart to illustrate the steps involved. This visual representation helps the audience see the process at a glance and understand how each part fits together.

Follow-up and Community Impact

Creating Vivid Value isn't just about a single act of giving; it's about a continuous process with the potential for long-term impact. Follow-up and considering the broader community context are crucial to ensure your actions truly create lasting, positive change.

Sustaining impact involves checking in with the recipient after offering help. Did your actions achieve their intended outcome? For example, if you provided support to a colleague on a project, follow up to see whether they are finding the tools and strategies useful. Offering additional support if needed can ensure the long-term success of your initial efforts, fostering a sense of partnership and ensuring sustained impact.

Feedback and growth are essential components of this process. Use follow-up as an opportunity to learn and improve. Ask the recipient for feedback on your approach or suggestions for how you can be more helpful in the future. This self-reflection allows you to refine your skills and provide even greater Vivid Value in future interactions. For instance, after conducting a workshop, gathering participants' feedback can help you adjust and enhance future sessions.

I am in no way perfect at the gifts and superpowers I am offering others. Even when I am delivering any kind of value to others, I know there are likely things I could have done differently or better. For example, I am usually not the one on stage giving presentations, but I have wanted to develop and refine that as a skill. Once, I gave a presentation at a conference to a user group that could be potential clients. After I wrapped it up, I went to those I knew in the audience and asked for their feedback—what they liked, what they felt could have been different, where they felt lost. I used that feedback to improve for the next time I would present.

I apply the same approach when counseling individuals from my church. I go with what my heart is telling me to say to them and then review it with our bishop. I run through the scenario and what was said and always ask for his thoughts and feedback. This consistent follow-up has significantly amplified the impact of my initial acts of giving. By seeking feedback and reflecting on my performance, I can continue to build on the value I am offering others.

Identifying systemic issues is also crucial when offering help. When you're consistently delivering value, patterns often emerge that point to deeper, underlying challenges. These systemic issues might not be immediately visible, but addressing them can create lasting, meaningful change.

Think of it like helping someone organize their desk repeatedly. While the immediate value is clear—a tidy workspace—the deeper issue might be a lack of organizational systems or time management skills. By looking beyond the surface-level problem, you can offer more impactful solutions that create lasting change.

Consider whether there are underlying causes that need to be addressed. Ask yourself:

- What keeps causing this issue to resurface?
- Are there common themes in the challenges people face?
- What resources or skills are consistently missing?
- How could addressing the root cause prevent future problems?

For example, if you're helping small business owners streamline their operations, you might notice that many struggle with the same technology challenges. Instead of just fixing individual problems, you could develop a basic training program that helps multiple business owners overcome these common hurdles.

Advocate for additional resources or identify gaps that need to be filled. This might mean:

- Connecting people with existing resources they don't know about

- Building networks of support within communities
- Creating new solutions where none exist
- Bringing attention to overlooked needs

For instance, if you notice recurring issues in a community project, work toward addressing these root causes to create a more sustainable and long-term solution. Maybe volunteers keep dropping out because they feel overwhelmed. Rather than constantly recruiting new volunteers, you might develop a better onboarding process, create smaller, more manageable tasks, or implement a buddy system for support.

Remember, creating vivid value isn't just about solving immediate problems—it's about making lasting improvements that continue to benefit others long after your initial involvement. When you address systemic issues, your impact multiplies, touching not just individuals but entire communities or organizations.

By taking this deeper approach to value creation, you transform one-time fixes into ongoing solutions. This is how your gifts and superpowers can create ripple effects that continue to grow and expand, inviting even more opportunities for the universe to pay you back.

The Power of Gratitude

Acknowledgement and appreciation are foundational elements of gratitude. For instance, thanking someone for the opportunity to use your gifts and superpowers shows respect and acknowledges their situation. Imagine tutoring a student and expressing gratitude for their dedication and willingness to learn. This simple act creates a positive atmosphere and fosters a sense of mutual respect, making the learning experience more enjoyable and effective for both parties.

Shifting the focus through gratitude highlights the positive aspects of giving. Instead of solely concentrating on the problem being addressed, it emphasizes the potential for growth and learning. Suppose you're helping a friend clean their home. By expressing gratitude for their willingness to tackle the project, you create a more positive and collaborative experience. This shift in focus can change a mundane task into a shared, uplifting activity.

When working with individuals one-on-one to help them build a plan for self-reliance, it's not uncommon for them to feel down about their situation. They often make self-deprecating statements, which can hinder their progress. To combat this, I always start by acknowledging the difficulty of the conversation and thanking them for their willingness to open up.

Expressing gratitude in this way often puts the person at ease and makes them more receptive to the value I am offering. For example, during one session, a client began to speak negatively about their situation. I immediately expressed my gratitude for their honesty and willingness to share their feelings. This simple act of appreciation helped them feel more comfortable and validated.

As we continued our conversation, they made another self-critical comment. I took the opportunity to remind them that being open about their emotions is a step forward, and I thanked them again for their honesty. This consistent expression of gratitude helped build a deeper level of trust between us.

Expressing gratitude not only enhances the giving experience but also reinforces the value being given. It creates a feedback loop of positivity and appreciation, strengthening the bond between giver and receiver and making the act of giving more fulfilling.

Exercise 1: Personalization Challenge

Purpose: Customize your next act of giving based on the recipient's specific needs or desires.

Instructions:

- Identify Recipient: Write down the name of the recipient and their specific needs or preferences.

- Brainstorm Personalization: List personalized touches you can add to your act of giving. Think about small, thoughtful details that would make your gesture stand out.

- Document Outcome: Record the process and outcome of your personalized act of giving. Reflect on how the recipient responded and the impact it had on your relationship.

Tip: Consider what would make the recipient feel truly seen and appreciated.

Exercise 2: Storytelling Exercise

Purpose: Craft a story around your value offering, focusing on emotional engagement and impact.

Instructions:

- Outline Your Story: Use the provided sections to outline the beginning, middle, and end of your story. Ensure your story is clear, engaging, and relatable.

- Engage Emotionally: Identify the key emotions you want to evoke in your audience. Think about how your story can connect on an emotional level.

- Craft Your Message: Write the core message of your story that highlights the value you are providing. Ensure your message is impactful and memorable.

Tip: Use personal anecdotes and relatable examples to make your story more engaging.

Exercise 3: Visual Impact Project

Purpose: Enhance the presentation of your value offering using visual elements.

Instructions:

- Brainstorm Visual Ideas: List ideas for enhancing the visual presentation of your value offering. Consider elements like colors, packaging, branding, and layout.

- Plan Implementation: Detail how you will implement these visual ideas. Create a step-by-step plan to ensure effective execution.

- Gather Feedback: Document any feedback received and note any adjustments needed. Reflect on how visual enhancements impacted the recipient's experience.

Tip: Use visuals that are clear, compelling, and align with your message.

Exercises and Actionable Content

This chapter's exercises are designed to boost your storytelling, experiential value design, visual impact, and more.

You can access the Chapter 7 worksheet by going to www.thegivermethod.com/chapter-7-worksheets

Chapter 8: Engagements

Engaging with Your Gifts and Superpowers

"Reflect upon your present blessings, of which every man has plenty; not on your past misfortunes, of which all men have some." - Charles Dickens

---

A few years back, I attended a conference in Toronto, Canada. I had been there a few days and had the opportunity to interact with and engage with many of the attendees. One attendee, in particular, asked if I could help her solve a few issues she was having with her business. We sat in the hotel lobby and walked through how she talked about her services and what she could do differently to connect with more individuals.

After I helped her out, she asked if she could help me with anything. At the time, I was struggling with imposter syndrome and trying to become better at communicating. I asked if there was anything she saw that I could work on, and she immediately pointed out that I seemed uncomfortable around more established members of the group and struggled with maintaining eye contact.

We took the time to talk through it. She even drew out a little diagram to help me visualize what she was sharing. In this engagement, we both were able to share our gifts and superpowers to help each other. We both walked away feeling a deeper connection.

Every engagement will be different, but the more you focus on the lessons learned throughout this book, the better each engagement will feel.

Understanding Engagements

Engagements are interactions in which you utilize your gifts and superpowers to intentionally and impactfully influence others by delivering vivid value. These engagements can range from personal conversations to public speaking events, workshops, or community activities. The key is to be present, curious, and committed to creating a meaningful connection.

Engagements can be broadly categorized into two types: one-to-one interactions and one-to-many interactions. Each type has its unique characteristics and requires different approaches to maximize their impact.

One-to-One Interactions

One-to-one interactions are deeply personal and provide an opportunity to connect on an individual level.

These engagements can be incredibly powerful when you tailor your approach to meet the specific needs of the person you're interacting with.

Mentorship Sessions: Offering personalized guidance and support can significantly impact someone's growth and development. Imagine sitting down with a mentee who is navigating a career change. By actively listening, asking insightful questions, and sharing your own experiences, you can provide the direction and encouragement they need to take the next step confidently. Understanding this type of engagement is crucial as it allows you to create personalized growth experiences, potentially shaping someone's future in profound ways.

Personal Conversations: Deep, meaningful discussions that address individual needs can strengthen relationships and foster trust. Picture a heartfelt conversation with a friend who is going through a tough time. By being fully present, empathetic, and offering a listening ear, you create a safe space for them to express their feelings and find solace in your support. Recognizing the value of these interactions helps you build deeper, more meaningful relationships and become a trusted confidant in times of need.

Coaching: Tailored advice to help someone improve or achieve a goal can be transformative. Think of a scenario where you coach a colleague on improving their presentation skills. By providing constructive feedback, demonstrating techniques, and offering encouragement, you help them build confidence and deliver a more impactful presentation. Understanding the coaching dynamic is important as it enables you to effectively guide others towards their goals, helping them unlock their full potential.

One-to-Many Interactions

One-to-many interactions allow you to reach and influence a larger audience. These engagements require a different set of skills to ensure your message resonates with a diverse group of people.

Workshops and Seminars: Educational sessions designed for a group can empower participants with new knowledge and skills. Consider leading a workshop on effective communication skills. By incorporating interactive activities, real-life examples, and practical tips, you engage the audience and provide valuable takeaways. Understanding how to conduct these sessions effectively allows you to share your knowledge more broadly, potentially creating an automatic force for positive change.

Public Speaking: Sharing knowledge and inspiring a large audience can have a profound impact. Picture yourself giving a keynote speech at a conference. By weaving personal stories, compelling visuals, and a clear, passionate message, you captivate the audience and leave them motivated to take action. Grasping the nuances of public speaking is vital as it empowers you to inspire and motivate large groups, amplifying your impact exponentially.

Community Events: Activities that involve and benefit the community at large can foster a sense of belonging and collective impact. Imagine organizing a community clean-up event. By rallying volunteers, coordinating logistics, and highlighting the positive impact on the neighborhood, your actions spark a more active and diverse community. Understanding how to organize and lead these events allows you to foster a sense of unity and shared purpose.

Any engagement can be a good engagement, but some can turn out to be negative. Sometimes, it's the smallest things that can change how we view the situation. Let me share two quick stories that highlight this point.

Years ago, at the company I worked at, we invited a specialist to our office who was renowned for helping companies tell their story for branding purposes. We had an eight-hour session scheduled with him. The day began with him teaching us all the concepts of storytelling, which took up about seven hours. This left us with only one hour to actually dive into the work and create the magic of our story. We were all a bit let down by the day's results and it took time before we really felt the value of what he was teaching.

In contrast, not too long ago, we worked with another specialist on scaling group programs. Before we could do our onboarding call with them, we had to watch specific videos and complete some worksheets. These tools helped us organize our thinking so that when we got on the onboarding call, we could hit the ground running. We immediately felt the value and were excited to engage more.

Both specialists are amazing at what they do and provide tremendous value to their clients. Unlike the first interaction, the second engagement left us feeling energized and excited thanks to the specialist's meticulous pre-call preparation. By helping us see the bigger picture and equipping us with what we needed to be successful, the second specialist was able to provide more value and a more meaningful impact.

Interestingly, since working with the first specialist, he has also adopted a similar onboarding approach as the second specialist. This adjustment allows his clients to get started faster and feel the value and excitement immediately.

> These experiences taught me that the key difference between a positive and a negative engagement often lies in the preparation and intentionality behind it.

When you help someone see the bigger picture and give them the tools they need to be successful, you can provide more value and impact.

The Power of Listening

Active listening is a superpower in itself. It demonstrates genuine interest, builds trust, and fosters a positive engagement. By truly listening, you show the other person that they are valued and understood, creating a deeper connection that can significantly enhance the impact of your engagements.

Imagine you're having a conversation with a colleague who is sharing their concerns about a project. By putting away your phone, maintaining eye contact, and fully engaging in the conversation, you convey that their words are important to you. This simple act of minimizing distractions can make a world of difference in how the other person perceives the interaction.

Minimize Distractions: The first step in active listening is to eliminate any distractions that might divert your attention. When you put away your phone and focus entirely on the person speaking, you show respect and genuine interest. This creates a space where the other person feels safe and valued. Common distractions might include notifications on your devices, background noise in busy environments, or even your own internal thoughts and worries. It's also easy to get distracted by thinking about what you'll say next instead of fully focusing on the speaker's words. Recognizing and actively working to minimize these distractions can significantly improve the quality of your listening and the depth of your engagements.

Verbal and Non-Verbal Cues: Expressing attentiveness through verbal and non-verbal cues can significantly enhance your listening skills. Simple gestures like nodding, smiling, and using encouraging phrases such as "I see" or "That's interesting" show that you are engaged and following the conversation. These cues reinforce that you are present and actively involved in the interaction.

Ask Clarifying Questions: To truly understand what's being said, it's essential to ask clarifying questions. Paraphrasing the speaker's words and asking thoughtful questions not only ensures clarity but also shows that you are genuinely interested in their perspective. For example, you might say, "So what you're saying is..." or "Can you elaborate on that?" This practice helps deepen your understanding and makes the speaker feel heard and valued.

Empathy Over Sympathy: Putting yourself in the speaker's shoes and understanding their emotions is a crucial aspect of active listening. Empathy involves feeling with the person and acknowledging their experiences, while sympathy might simply convey pity. By showing empathy, you validate their feelings and build a stronger emotional connection. For instance, if a friend is sharing a difficult experience, you could respond with, "I can imagine how tough that must be for you."

Resist the Urge to Interrupt: One of the most challenging aspects of active listening is resisting the urge to interrupt. Allow the speaker to express their thoughts fully without interjecting your own opinions or solutions. This patience demonstrates respect and gives the speaker the space to articulate their ideas. Interruptions can disrupt the flow of conversation and make the speaker feel undervalued.

Active listening is not just about hearing words; it's about understanding and connecting with the person speaking. I recently had a powerful reminder of the power of listening. It happened during a call with a former client who had left our services somewhat dissatisfied. I wanted to understand her perspective and see what I could do to help her feel better about her time working with us.

She began by explaining her experience, detailing where her expectations had not been met, and expressing how it made her feel. As she spoke, I listened to her words but was already planning my response. When it was my turn to talk, I launched into a lengthy explanation of how things had changed and what was different now. I was so focused on my own points that I didn't pay attention to her responses, facial expressions, or body language.

After I finished my monologue, she asked me if I felt that what I said addressed her concerns. She also pointed out that I hadn't noticed how she was showing up in the conversation. She suggested that I watch the recording of our call to see if I could tell how she was feeling.

Later on, I did just that. As I watched the recording, it became painfully clear that she had been completely unengaged in the conversation. Nothing I said seemed to resonate with her. I realized that I hadn't truly listened to her. I had missed the mark on so many levels, trying to make her feel better about her experience without genuinely addressing her concerns.

This experience was a humbling lesson. It showed me how crucial active listening is in any engagement. By failing to truly listen, I missed the opportunity to connect with her and address her concerns meaningfully. Engaging in active listening can dramatically shift the tone and direction of your conversations. It can upgrade a disengaged conversation into a meaningful exchange where both parties feel heard and valued. This simple act of truly listening can make a world of difference in the outcome of any engagement.

Emotional Intelligence

Before we dive in, I want to make it clear that I'm not claiming to be an expert on emotional intelligence. There's a wealth of resources out there on this topic, written by researchers and professionals who've spent years studying it. What I'm offering here is my perspective on how emotional intelligence aligns with engagements and the GIVER Method, based on my experiences and understanding. I'll do my best to show you how this concept can enhance your ability to connect with others and make a positive impact.

Emotional intelligence (EQ) is the ability to understand and manage your own emotions, as well as recognize and influence the emotions of others. It plays a crucial role in creating effective engagements and fostering positive relationships. Developing your EQ can significantly enhance your interactions, allowing you to connect more deeply and respond more effectively.

Self-Awareness: This is the foundation of emotional intelligence. Self-awareness involves recognizing your own emotions and understanding how they impact your thoughts and behavior. For example, if you notice that you're feeling anxious before a big presentation, acknowledging this emotion can help you address it constructively, perhaps through deep breathing or positive self-talk.

Self-Regulation: Once you're aware of your emotions, the next step is managing them. Self-regulation means controlling your emotional responses and maintaining composure under stress. Imagine you're in a heated meeting where tensions are high. Instead of reacting impulsively, taking a moment to pause and respond calmly can prevent escalation and keep the discussion productive.

Motivation: High EQ individuals are driven by internal rewards and meaningful goals. They stay motivated even in the face of challenges. For instance, if you're working on a long-term project, focusing on the personal and professional growth it offers can keep you motivated, even during tough times.

Empathy: Empathy is the ability to understand and share the feelings of others. It allows you to connect with people on a deeper level and respond to their needs more effectively. When a colleague confides in you about a personal struggle, showing empathy—truly listening and offering support—can strengthen your relationship and make them feel valued and understood.

Social Skills: Building relationships and navigating social situations effectively are key components of EQ.

Good social skills involve clear communication, conflict resolution, and teamwork. Whether you're leading a team or participating in a group project, strong social skills help you collaborate effectively and create a positive work environment.

Emotional intelligence plays a crucial role in many aspects of life, especially in high-emotion engagements. Let me share a real-life example from my experience that highlights its significance.

Through involvement with my church, I've often had to counsel individuals facing marital issues. These situations are emotionally charged, with both parties expressing intense feelings about why they think they're right and what the other side has done wrong. Navigating these conversations requires a high level of emotional intelligence.

During these sessions, I have to ensure that I'm not making assumptions about either side. It's essential to remain neutral and not take sides. Building a trusting relationship is one of the biggest parts of the GIVER Method, as it allows me to guide the conversation constructively. I use empathy to understand each person's perspective, ensuring they feel heard and valued.

Emotional intelligence helps me keep a clear head amidst the emotional turmoil. By focusing on the overall goal of the engagement, which is to provide guidance and support, I can steer the conversation towards resolution and understanding. It's about balancing empathy with clear-headed thinking, ensuring that my advice is both compassionate and practical.

In these counseling sessions, emotional intelligence allows me to connect deeply with the individuals involved. They need to feel heard and understood for any advice to resonate and be effective. While not all engagements are as intense as marital counseling, the principles of emotional intelligence—empathy, active listening, and maintaining emotional balance—are equally important in all types of interactions.

Example of EQ in Action: Consider a scenario where you're leading a team through a challenging project. One of your team members, Alex, seems unusually quiet and disengaged during meetings. Instead of assuming Alex is simply uninterested, you decide to apply your emotional intelligence skills. First, you use self-awareness to recognize any assumptions you might be making and self-regulation to approach Alex calmly and without judgment. You then have a private conversation with Alex, where you practice empathy by asking open-ended questions and actively listening to their concerns.

Alex opens up about feeling overwhelmed and underappreciated. You use your social skills to acknowledge Alex's feelings and discuss ways to support them better, such as redistributing workload or providing more regular feedback. Your motivation to maintain a positive team environment drives you to follow up on these changes, ensuring Alex feels more valued and engaged.

This approach not only helps Alex feel heard and supported but also strengthens the overall team's morale and productivity. By leveraging your emotional intelligence, you turn a potential issue into an opportunity for growth and improvement.

Adaptability

Adaptability is the ability to adjust your approach based on the specific engagement and the people involved. It's crucial for maximizing the impact of your gifts and superpowers. By staying flexible and open to change, you can tailor your interactions to meet the needs of different individuals and situations.

Imagine you're giving a presentation to a diverse audience. Some attendees might prefer detailed data and analysis, while others might resonate more with personal stories and anecdotes. Being adaptable means you can shift your approach on the fly, incorporating both elements to keep everyone engaged and interested.

Stay Open-Minded: Adaptability starts with an open mind. Be willing to consider different perspectives and approaches, even if they differ from your own. This openness allows you to see situations from various angles and find the best way to connect with your audience. For example, during a team meeting, you might encounter conflicting ideas. Instead of dismissing them, consider how each perspective could contribute to a better solution.

Continuously Learn: Expanding your skills and techniques keeps you versatile. The more you know, the better equipped you are to handle different scenarios. Take courses, attend workshops, and read widely to stay updated in your field. An example of this is learning about new communication strategies or leadership styles can provide fresh tools to enhance your engagements.

Observe and Reflect: After each engagement, take time to analyze what went well and what could be improved. Reflecting on your interactions helps you refine your approach for future engagements. Maybe you noticed that a particular story resonated well with your audience, or that certain questions helped facilitate deeper discussions. Use these insights to adjust your methods and enhance your impact.

Practice Empathy: Understanding others' needs, preferences, and feelings is key to adaptability. Empathy allows you to connect on a deeper level and tailor your approach to be more effective. When you truly understand where someone is coming from, you can adjust your communication style to meet their needs. For example, if a colleague is feeling stressed, you might offer support and encouragement rather than additional tasks.

Be Proactive: Anticipate changes and plan for flexibility. Having a backup plan or alternative strategy ensures you can adapt when unexpected challenges arise. For instance, if you're leading a workshop and the technology fails, being prepared with offline activities or discussions can keep the session productive.

Adaptability is a critical skill that I utilize daily in my engagements, particularly when working with clients. Each interaction presents new and diverse challenges, often driven by the client's unique goals and motivations, which may differ significantly from my own. My primary objective is to help organize their thinking to create an executable plan, but their priorities can vary widely. Some clients are focused on getting things done quickly, others want to learn different parts of the process, and some are only interested in the end result, regardless of the organization.

I might have a client who is in a hurry to see results and has little patience for detailed planning. In such cases, I adapt by streamlining our discussions, focusing on immediate action steps, and delivering quick wins to build momentum. Conversely, with a client eager to understand the intricacies of the process, I take a more educational approach, breaking down each step and explaining the rationale behind our actions to ensure they feel knowledgeable and empowered.

Adaptability isn't limited to client interactions. Whether you are a sales rep taking calls, working the front desk and greeting people, or managing relationships with spouses, children, family, and friends, each engagement requires a tailored approach. The ability to shift your focus and strategies to meet the specific needs of those you're interacting with is essential.

Being adaptable also means being intentional with your engagements. It involves understanding and responding to the needs of others, serving them with your gifts and superpowers. For instance, with a client who values efficiency, I might use quick, clear communication and provide concise updates. For someone who appreciates detail, I would ensure thorough explanations and more frequent check-ins.

Improving Social Interactions

Social interactions are the foundation of engagements. How we connect with others, whether in personal or professional settings, can significantly impact the quality of our relationships and the effectiveness of our engagements. Improving your social skills not only helps in building stronger connections but also enhances your ability to deliver value using your gifts and superpowers.

I have not always been good at communicating. In fact, I got so bad at it that I started to avoid making eye contact with individuals while talking to them. I couldn't explain it; one day, I just realized that my communication had deteriorated, and the lack of eye contact only made things more awkward.

I set a goal to develop the gift of communication. It started small by focusing on my daily written and verbal interactions. I would set little goals for the day and then review them to see how I did, documenting where I was struggling. I began to notice more when I wasn't making eye contact with individuals. This did not change overnight; it took almost a year of daily focus to see significant improvement.

Now, when you hear that it took almost a year, you might think, "Wow, that's a long time," and it is! But it didn't feel like it because I was celebrating every little win along the way. I celebrated after interactions with my team members, I celebrated when I communicated better with my wife and boys, and I celebrated the first time in years I was able to maintain eye contact with someone throughout an entire conversation. The bigger win I celebrated from that was finding a deeper connection with the person I spoke to, as it felt more engaging.

Here are some essential tips to elevate your social interactions:

Ask Open-Ended Questions: Encouraging others to talk about themselves can deepen your connections and provide valuable insights into their thoughts and feelings. Open-ended questions—those that can't be answered with a simple "yes" or "no"—invite more detailed responses. Questions like "What inspired you to take this path?" or "How do you feel about the current project?" show genuine interest and can lead to richer, more meaningful conversations.

Maintain Eye Contact: Eye contact is a powerful tool in communication. It shows that you are engaged, confident, and interested in what the other person is saying. Maintaining eye contact can help establish a connection and build rapport. The key to effective eye contact is striking a balance to ensure clear communication without causing discomfort. A good rule of thumb is to maintain eye contact for about 60-70% of the conversation.

Observe Body Language: Nonverbal cues can provide significant insights into what others are feeling and expressing. Paying attention to body language—such as facial expressions, gestures, and posture—can help you better understand the unspoken elements of a conversation. For instance, crossed arms might indicate defensiveness, while leaning in could show interest and engagement. Being aware of these cues allows you to respond more effectively and empathetically.

Example of Social Interaction Improvement: Imagine you're attending a networking event, a setting that can sometimes feel intimidating. Instead of sticking to safe, surface-level topics, you decide to practice empathy and active listening. You approach a fellow attendee who seems a bit reserved and strike up a conversation with an open-ended question like, "What brings you to this event?" As they begin to share, you maintain eye contact, nod, and occasionally paraphrase what they're saying to show that you're truly listening.

You notice that they relax and open up more, sharing their professional experiences and personal interests. You also pay attention to their body language, noticing when they lean in, signaling their engagement in the conversation. By being present, showing genuine interest, and responding empathetically, you not only make the other person feel valued but also create a meaningful connection that could lead to future collaborations.

Exercises and Actionable Content

This chapter's activities are crafted to help you reflect on past experiences, plan future engagements, and continuously improve the impact you have on those you influence. By engaging deeply with these exercises, you'll be better equipped to make meaningful and lasting connections, reinforcing your journey to becoming a true GIVER.

You can access the Chapter 8 worksheet by going to www.thegivermethod.com/chapter-8-worksheets

Chapter 9:
Make Engagements Effective and Eager

Eager Engagements and Meaningful Interactions

"I've learned that people will forget what you said, people will forget what you did, but people will never forget how you made them feel." – Maya Angelou

---

A few months ago, I was on a group coaching/mastermind call. During the session, someone mentioned a struggle they were facing, and I knew I could provide some valuable insights. I offered to have a separate call with them to review different strategies and ideas they could implement. We scheduled the call, and I prepared thoroughly, ensuring I had relevant information and actionable steps ready to share.

During our call, I walked them through various strategies and ideas tailored to their situation. We discussed practical ways they could address their challenges, and I made sure to listen attentively to their concerns and questions. By the end of the call, they felt equipped with new tools and perspectives to tackle their issues. We wrapped up our conversation and went our separate ways for the time being.

About a month later, we both attended the same event. I arrived at the event eager to learn and ready to serve those I could. When I ran into them at the event, they stopped me and said, "I have been looking all over for you. I couldn't wait to see you and catch up." We proceeded to talk about how things were going, and eventually, they said, "Thank you for taking that time with me last month. I took it to heart and have implemented it into my business, and I am already seeing results."

Although there are technically two engagements here, the one I want to focus on is the second one. They were excited to see me and had been looking forward to our interaction. They wanted to share the results of what we discussed and how they had implemented my suggestions. This is a perfect example of how engagements can be eager. Eager engagement happens when people look forward to interacting with you because of the value you bring with your gifts and superpowers.

Reflecting on this experience, here are some key elements that made this engagement stand out:

Preparation and Execution: I took specific actions to prepare thoroughly for the call, ensuring I had relevant information and actionable steps ready to share. This preparation helped make the engagement effective.

Response and Feedback: The other person responded positively to my approach, actively engaging in the conversation and implementing the strategies we discussed. Their excitement to see me at the event and their feedback about the positive results they experienced were incredibly rewarding.

Lessons Learned: This experience reinforced the importance of preparation, advanced active listening, and providing tailored, actionable advice. It showed me how impactful my gifts and superpowers could be when used to serve others. I learned that creating value in my engagements could lead to eager and enthusiastic interactions, where people look forward to connecting with me again.

By focusing on these elements, you too can create eager and effective engagements, making a lasting positive impact on those you interact with.

A quote I love is, "Everyone you will ever meet knows something you don't." – Bill Nye (the Science Guy). Each engagement is an opportunity to learn and grow. Embrace every interaction with curiosity and an open mind, knowing that both you and the other person have valuable insights to share.

Enhancing Engagements and Interactions

In previous chapters, you learned the importance of active listening, empathy, personalized communication, and shared experiences. Developing these skills further will make your engagements more eager and effective. Let's discuss how these strategies can be applied within the GIVER Method to enhance the quality and impact of every interaction.

To enhance your interactions, let's dive into advanced active listening techniques and empathetic communication strategies. Consider using reflective listening to confirm understanding, where you paraphrase and reflect back what the speaker has said to ensure clarity and demonstrate that you are truly listening. This can involve asking deeper questions that prompt the other person to elaborate, creating a richer dialogue.

Another advanced technique is empathic accuracy, which involves honing in on and understanding the emotional undertones of what the other person is saying. It's about picking up on subtle cues and nonverbal signals, and then validating those emotions in your response. For instance, if a colleague shares their struggles with a project, recognizing not just the factual content but also the frustration or stress behind their words can help you respond with greater empathy.

Personalized communication is about tailoring your message to fit the needs and preferences of the person you're engaging with. This means considering their communication style, interests, and current state of mind. For example, if you know someone prefers visual aids, try incorporating more charts and diagrams in your presentation. This small adjustment can make your message more impactful and easier to understand.

Shared experiences are powerful because they create common ground. When you share stories or experiences, you're not just exchanging information; you're connecting on a human level. Think about a time when you bonded with someone over a shared challenge or triumph. Those moments of connection can make your engagements more memorable and meaningful.

By integrating these strategies into your interactions, you'll find that your engagements become more effective and leave a lasting positive impression. Each conversation, meeting, or presentation is an opportunity to practice these skills and enhance your influence. Embrace the journey of continuous improvement and watch as your engagements become more impactful and rewarding.

Effective Engagements

Engagements can range from being highly impactful and positive to being negative and forgettable. Understanding what makes an engagement effective can help you maximize the impact of your interactions.

Effective engagements are characterized by two-way communication, where both parties actively participate and exchange ideas. This creates a more engaging interaction. For instance, instead of delivering a monologue, ask questions and invite feedback. This not only makes the other person feel valued but also enriches the conversation.

Personalized value is another key component. Tailor your approach to address the specific needs and interests of the person you're engaging with. Think about a time when someone took the effort to understand your unique situation and offered tailored advice. It felt more meaningful, didn't it? By customizing your message, you ensure that your engagement resonates on a deeper level.

Provide actionable insights. Offer practical advice or tools that the recipient can immediately apply. This not only demonstrates your expertise but also helps the other person see tangible benefits from the interaction. Imagine attending a workshop where you leave with clear, actionable steps. It's far more valuable than just theoretical knowledge.

Building a memorable connection is crucial. When you connect with someone on a personal level, the engagement leaves a lasting impression. Share stories, show empathy, and be genuinely interested in the other person. Create a safe and open space for communication. When people feel comfortable, they're more likely to engage fully and share openly. These elements create a bond that goes beyond the immediate interaction.

Be adaptable. Each person has a different learning style and preference. Adjust your approach to meet their needs. Whether it's through visual aids, storytelling, or hands-on activities, find what works best for them.

Eager to Engage

Creating eager engagements means making others genuinely excited to interact with you. This happens when they recognize your expertise and credibility. Your knowledge and skills make you a valuable resource, and they trust that you can provide insights that will benefit them. Think about how you feel when you consult with an expert whose advice you respect. Their credibility makes you more inclined to listen and engage.

Passion and enthusiasm are contagious. When you are genuinely passionate about your subject, it naturally draws people in. Your excitement makes your message more compelling. Reflect on a time when someone's enthusiasm inspired you.

A focus on solutions is crucial. People appreciate practical advice that addresses their challenges. When you offer clear, actionable solutions, it shows that you understand their needs and are capable of helping them.

Your empowering approach can leave others feeling capable and motivated. When your interactions boost their confidence and provide them with tools to succeed, they are more likely to seek out future engagements. Think about how good it feels when someone helps you feel empowered and capable.

Creating an uplifting atmosphere makes people feel comfortable and valued. A welcoming demeanor encourages open communication and makes others feel at ease. Remember a time when someone's positivity made you feel more relaxed and engaged. That kind of environment fosters eager participation.

To spark eager engagements, focus on developing your expertise. Continuously improve your skills and knowledge to stay relevant and valuable. This ongoing growth not only enhances your credibility but also keeps you excited about your field.

Emphasize the benefits of engaging with you. Clearly communicate the positive outcomes people can achieve.

Highlight how your insights or assistance can make a tangible difference in their lives or work.

Authentic communication is key. Be genuine and transparent in your interactions. People appreciate honesty and can quickly sense insincerity. By being yourself, you build trust and encourage more meaningful connections.

Encourage open communication and participation. Create an interactive environment where people feel comfortable sharing their thoughts and ideas. This collaboration enhances the quality of the engagement.

Celebrate successes. Recognize and highlight the achievements of those who have benefited from your help. This not only validates their efforts but also reinforces the value of engaging with you.

Overcoming Communication Barriers

Distractions are a major hindrance to effective communication. To minimize external distractions, choose a quiet environment where you can focus without interruptions. Limiting multitasking is also important. If you're trying to do several things at once, your attention is divided, and the quality of your communication suffers. Internal distractions, such as wandering thoughts or stress, can also disrupt your focus. Practicing mindfulness techniques, like deep breathing or brief meditation, can help you stay present in the conversation.

Interrupting can derail the flow of communication and make the other person feel undervalued. Practicing advanced active listening is essential. This involves not just hearing the words, but fully understanding and interpreting the underlying emotions and intentions. For instance, using techniques like mirroring, where you repeat back what the other person has said in your own words, can help ensure that you are truly on the same page. It shows respect and ensures your reply is relevant and thoughtful. Using respectful verbal cues can help you interject appropriately without cutting the other person off.

A lack of clarity can lead to misunderstandings and frustration. Tailoring your communication to your audience needs to be your focus. Use language and examples that are relevant and easy for them to understand. Additionally, presenting your thoughts in a clear structure—beginning, middle, and end—helps convey your message more effectively. Organizing your ideas logically ensures that the listener can follow along and grasp your points.

Cultural differences can also pose a challenge in communication. Understanding norms around communication styles and nonverbal cues in different cultures can help prevent misunderstandings. If language barriers exist, utilizing translation services or finding an interpreter can facilitate clearer communication.

Remember, surrounding yourself with people who lift you higher, as Oprah Winfrey suggests, also means fostering an environment of clear and respectful communication. I've been coaching small businesses for over 10 years on how they can organize their thinking and create amazing client processes. Every business I work with is unique—they sell different products, come from diverse backgrounds, are at various stages of development, and are located all over the world. Early on, I realized that to be effective, I needed to be intentional about managing these barriers. One common challenge was dealing with distractions. Business owners often attend events or mastermind groups where they get bombarded with ideas, which can derail our coaching focus. To address this, I created a "distraction journal" where they can jot down these ideas to review later, ensuring we stay on track during our sessions.

Interruptions from team members or family during coaching calls were another frequent issue. I started emphasizing the importance of setting aside uninterrupted time for our calls. If a client continuously faced interruptions, I insisted on rescheduling to a time when they could be in a quieter environment. This approach helped create a more focused and productive session.

Clarity issues also posed a significant barrier. Business owners often didn't know exactly what they needed to discuss or how to address their challenges. To combat this, I began requiring them to send over pre-meeting agendas outlining the topics they wanted to cover. This preparation not only brought more clarity to our discussions but also ensured they came to the call with a clear focus.

The Power of Enthusiasm

Imagine explaining your area of expertise with a monotone voice and closed-off body language. Does that sound like a recipe for an eager engagement? Absolutely not! Genuine enthusiasm is the secret sauce that upgrades an ordinary interaction into a captivating and memorable experience.

When you're genuinely excited about what you're discussing, your enthusiasm draws people in and ignites their desire to learn and engage. This excitement is infectious and can turn a mundane conversation into a lively and engaging experience.

An enthusiastic demeanor also helps create a positive atmosphere. People feel more comfortable and valued when they sense your genuine interest and excitement. This positive environment encourages open communication and makes others more willing to participate and share their thoughts.

Enthusiasm enhances clarity and focus in your delivery. When you're passionate about a topic, you naturally emphasize key points. Your energy helps highlight the most important aspects, ensuring that your audience retains the information.

Your enthusiasm builds trust and rapport. Passion demonstrates your commitment to the subject and to the people you're engaging with. It shows that you care deeply about what you're discussing and about their understanding and involvement. This commitment fosters trust, making your audience more receptive to your message.

As I've mentioned, I performed comedy for quite some time. Over the years, I often hosted shows, kicking things off and getting the crowd energized before the other performers took the stage. I was really good at it and could warm up a crowd quickly. My excitement and enthusiasm for entertaining people played a huge role. But this wasn't when I fully grasped the power of enthusiasm.

The real moment of clarity came during my daily work life. We often had multiple clients visiting the office at the same time. Before they broke off to work with their coaches, we would start with introductions and cover some basics about their time with us. I usually led these sessions but often felt awkward. The interactions felt fake and scripted, and I wanted to find a way to make everyone genuinely excited to be there.

That's when I thought about the tactics and techniques I used to warm up a comedy crowd. It dawned on me that it wasn't just the tactics but my genuine enthusiasm that got people engaged. The next week, when we had clients in, I decided to apply this insight. I kicked things off with the same intro items but did so with a genuine excitement for having them there and an enthusiastic outlook on the work they were about to do.

Remember, enthusiasm isn't about being loud or over-the-top. It's about conveying your genuine passion and excitement for the value you offer. By letting your enthusiasm shine through, you create a magnetic pull that draws others in.

Maintaining Authenticity

"The most important thing in communication is hearing what isn't said." – Peter Drucker. Consider how maintaining authenticity involves not just what you say, but also how you listen and respond to the unspoken needs and feelings of others. Your genuine engagement and attention to these subtleties can make a significant difference in your interactions.

Enthusiasm is essential for creating eager engagements, but it must be genuine. People can easily spot insincerity, and a forced performance can backfire, undermining your credibility and connection with others. Celebrate diversity by embracing your unique personality and perspective.

> Authenticity shines through when you are true to yourself, and it encourages others to do the same.

Maintaining authenticity involves focusing on genuine passion. Engage with topics that truly ignite your interest. Be transparent and humble, acknowledging your limitations and expressing a willingness to learn alongside others. Let curiosity lead the way. A lifelong learning mindset will naturally fuel your enthusiasm.

Embrace imperfections and don't be afraid to stumble or make minor mistakes. Being human and relatable fosters a sense of connection. Showing vulnerability can make your interactions more genuine and trustworthy.

Exercises and Actionable Content

This chapter's practice material includes an empathy challenge, engagement checklist, role-playing exercise, and more to amp up your interactions in any context.

You can access the Chapter 9 worksheet by going to www.thegivermethod.com/chapter-9-worksheets

Chapter 10:
Relationship Riches

Meaningful Relationship Riches Using Your Gifts

*"Why did you do all this for me?' he asked. 'I don't deserve it.
I've never done anything for you.' 'You have been my friend,'
replied Charlotte. 'That in itself is a tremendous thing.'"*
- E.B. White, Charlotte's Web

*"I used to think the worst thing in life was to end up all alone.
It's not. The worst thing in life is to end up with people that
make you feel all alone."*
- Robin Williams

Before I embraced being a GIVER, I used to withhold information, thinking it was the best way to protect my expertise and keep people dependent on me. In my work with clients, I would solve complex problems and, when asked how I did it, I would jokingly say, "Trade secrets" or "That's the magic you're paying for." While I was helping, I wasn't truly giving. I expected people to pay for my skills, and even then, I wasn't transparent about how things were done.

Everything changed after I adopted the GIVER Method. I realized that the more I shared and taught others, the stronger my relationships became. Now, my long-term clients are closer to me than ever because I am open about everything we do and how they can do it too. Relationship riches manifest in various ways, both in personal and professional life. The more you embrace being a GIVER, the more you will experience these positive outcomes in your relationships.

The GIVER Method and Relationships

At the heart of the GIVER Method is the powerful idea of giving without expecting anything in return. This selfless approach isn't just a strategy; it's a way of life that can enhance the way you interact with others. By embracing this philosophy, you can foster strong, meaningful relationships that thrive on trust, respect, and mutual growth.

When you focus on giving selflessly, you create an environment where people feel valued and appreciated. This kind of giving doesn't come with strings attached or hidden agendas. It's genuine, heartfelt, and impactful. Whether you're offering your time, skills, or support, your selflessness shines through, making others feel seen and understood.

In personal relationships, giving without expectation creates deeper, more resilient bonds that can weather any storm. In the workplace, a culture of selfless giving builds a network of trust and reliability. On a community level, selfless giving fosters a continuing sense of social responsibility and generosity.

The ultimate goal of The GIVER Method is to achieve meaningful relationship results. By practicing selfless giving, positively influencing others, creating value, and engaging deeply, you cultivate relationships that are built on trust, respect, and mutual growth in all spheres of life

How Selfless Giving Leads to Strong Relationships

Personal Relationships

Selfless giving is a cornerstone for nurturing and strengthening personal relationships. When you give to your loved ones without expecting anything in return, it sends a powerful message of genuine care and concern. This kind of giving shows that their happiness and well-being are your priority, not because you seek something in return, but because you truly value them.

In this environment of selflessness, trust naturally flourishes. Your loved ones feel safe knowing that your support and generosity come without hidden motives. This trust builds a strong foundation for your relationship, one where both parties feel secure and valued. Over time, this mutual respect and appreciation foster deeper emotional bonds, making the relationship more resilient to challenges and misunderstandings.

Imagine the impact of consistently giving your time, attention, and support to your partner, children, or friends. My boys and my wife may never truly know all the little things I do for them daily, and I don't need them to know. The bond between spouses or parents and children is built on countless selfless acts.

Reflecting on this makes me even more grateful for what my wife has done for me that I am unaware of and thankful for my parents and the countless selfless acts they must have performed throughout my life. These acts, though often unnoticed, form the foundation of our most cherished relationships, creating a deep well of trust, respect, and love that sustains us through life's challenges.

Professional Relationships

In the workplace, the principles of the GIVER Method can revolutionize how teams interact and collaborate. By focusing on giving value and supporting your colleagues, you create a professional environment built on trust and mutual respect. When you offer help, share knowledge, or provide resources without expecting immediate returns, you demonstrate reliability and commitment to the team's success.

This approach upgrades the workplace into a supportive network where everyone feels encouraged to contribute their best. Improved teamwork and collaboration become natural outcomes of such an environment. Colleagues are more likely to step up and assist each other, knowing that their efforts are reciprocated in spirit, if not immediately.

I hope that one day you can experience the kind of GIVER culture that has enriched my workplace for over eight years. Everyone is focused on building each other up. I've seen firsthand how offering help, sharing knowledge, and providing resources to my team have have produced an environment where everyone thrives together. And it starts with you.

Community and Social Connections

Whether it's through volunteering, participating in community projects, or simply offering a helping hand to neighbors, your selfless acts contribute to a culture of belonging. People are inspired by your actions and are often motivated to adopt similar behaviors. The more acts of generosity we observe, the more likely we are to believe that helping others is the norm. Generosity becomes the expected behavior. When kindness is consistently displayed, it sets a standard that others naturally follow, creating an environment where giving is a common practice.

Imagine a neighborhood where everyone follows the principles of the GIVER Method. Acts of kindness and support become the norm, leading to stronger social bonds and a more cohesive community. This environment not only enhances individual well-being but also creates a robust network of support that benefits everyone.

As I mentioned , I do a lot of work with my church. Currently, I serve in a role where I oversee all the men in our congregation. This position often makes me the go-to person when service is needed in our area. Whether it's helping with moves, yard work, or providing assistance to someone in need, there's always a demand for service.

I want those I serve with to see me working alongside them. This shared experience often helps create deeper relationships with those serving with me. I also understand the impact it has on those we are serving. Often, our efforts can be life-changing for individuals. I know that seeing a group of people willing to help can encourage others to ask for assistance, breaking through barriers of pride or hesitation.

Showing others that you are emotionally invested, that you are genuinely interested in their feelings and lived experiences, transforms any transactional relationship into one rooted in care and empathy.

Long-Term Impact on Relationships

When we give selflessly, we lay the groundwork for trust, connection, and mutual support that can last a lifetime. Genuine giving isn't about grand gestures or fleeting moments; it's about consistent, thoughtful acts that build a strong foundation for enduring relationships.

The beauty of this long-term impact lies in its compounding nature.

> Each act of giving, no matter how small, adds to the tapestry of your relationships. Over time, these acts weave together to create a strong, resilient bond that can weather life's storms.

It's like planting seeds of kindness and watching them grow into a flourishing garden of meaningful connections. A garden can become a legacy.

My high school drama teacher, Mr. Walsh, had a true passion for teaching and the performing arts. He was not just a teacher; he was a mentor who poured his heart and soul into every aspect of his work. He took our performances to levels beyond what we believed we could achieve. His dedication was evident in the literal blood, sweat, and tears he invested in the sets and productions we put on each year.

Mr. Walsh's commitment went far beyond the norm. He invested in us as individuals, ensuring that we understood the importance of hard work, creativity, and dedication. His passion was contagious, and he inspired us to push our boundaries and strive for excellence. Reflecting on his influence, I am amazed at how he managed to do this year after year.

Consider the impact of 30+ years of teaching, with two to four productions a year, each involving 25-50+ students, and the hundreds of attendees in the audience for one to six performances of each show. The sheer number of lives he touched is staggering. Hundreds, if not thousands, of Mr. Walsh's former students experienced his true passion for theater and the magic he brought to the classroom.

Mr. Walsh's dedication and investment in his students shaped my approach to relationships, emphasizing the value of deep, genuine investment in others. He showed me that the impact of our actions can extend far beyond our immediate circle and can create a lasting legacy of passion, commitment, and excellence. That is what I strive to emulate in my own life—giving fully and selflessly, knowing that it touches countless lives.

Building Trust

Trust Through Reciprocity: At the heart of any strong relationship is trust, and genuine giving plays a crucial role in building this trust. When you give without expecting anything in return, it creates a sense of security and appreciation in the relationship. Both parties feel comfortable giving and receiving. If you consistently offer your time and support to a friend in need, they will likely feel more inclined to do the same for you in the future.

Transparency and Honesty: Being honest and transparent in your interactions further strengthens trust. Open communication fosters an atmosphere of sincerity and reliability. For instance, sharing your true feelings and thoughts with a colleague, even when it's challenging, creates a more authentic and trustworthy working relationship. By being transparent, you show that you respect the other person enough to be honest, which in turn encourages them to do the same.

In no place is this more true than in a relationship with your significant other. For years, I struggled to share how I was feeling with my wife. This made communicating difficult at times. One night, we discussed it, and she described it as "failing to communicate about how you felt until it blew up in anger or over-the-top emotions." Once I was able to open up and actually start sharing my emotions, our connection grew stronger. We both feel completely comfortable sharing anything with each other now. Our honesty built a foundation of trust that has positively impacted the long-term dynamics of our relationship.

Creating Positive Memories and Shared History

In the past couple of years, my father-in-law passed away unexpectedly, and my uncle passed away after years of struggling with health issues. Leading up to each of their funerals, I was asked to give a blessing of comfort to someone close to them. For my father-in-law's funeral, it was my brother-in-law; for my uncle's funeral, it was my grandfather.

In both relationships, I never would have imagined being in a position where they would ask me to do this for them. I was deeply touched and honored to perform these blessings. Both instances took place during times of profound grief and pain. Despite the sorrow, I was able to see the change that came from giving these blessings. As I stood back after each blessing, I could feel the love coming from them and the immense gratitude they felt.

Every act of genuine giving creates positive memories and shared experiences that become integral parts of your relationship's history. These moments were not just acts of support but became lasting memories that will always be shared. They have drawn us closer to one another, creating a bond that continues to strengthen our relationships. Small acts of kindness, like giving a thoughtful gift or offering a listening ear, offer a similar purpose by incrementally producing a rich tapestry of shared experiences.

Exercises and Actionable Content

Now, it's time to take action and fully embrace your role as a GIVER. This chapter's resources help you visualize your connections, set goals, and track your progress using a relationship mapping tool, gratitude exercise, implementation brainstorm, and more.

You can access the Chapter 10 worksheet by going to www.thegivermethod.com/chapter-10-worksheets

---

Chapter 11:
Inviting the Universe
to Pay You Back

Embracing the Universe's Payback for Your Giving

*"The universe has this amazing way of giving back
to those who serve first."*
- Pat Flynn

Bob Proctor once said, "If you're not willing to do more than you are paid for you'll never be paid for more than you're doing. Giving is one of the laws of the universe. You've got to willingly give and graciously receive. And if you have to think before you give, you're trading—you're not giving." This wisdom underscores the essence of the GIVER Method: giving freely, without expecting anything in return, ultimately raises the tide for everyone, including yourself.

Your path began with Gifted (G), where you discovered and embraced your unique gifts and superpowers. This discovery laid the foundation for understanding your intrinsic value and how you can positively influence the world. You then moved to Influence (I), learning how to intentionally and impactfully influence others with your gifts. With this solid base, you advanced to Vivid Value (V), focusing on delivering meaningful value without expecting anything in return. Next, you explored Engagement (E), delving into the art of connecting deeply and effectively with others through empathy and trust. Finally, in Relationship Riches (R), you saw the culmination of your efforts in the form of strengthened, enriched relationships.

Now, having journeyed through these transformative stages, you are equipped to experience the universe's payback. Your growth from discovering your gifts to engaging eagerly and delivering vivid value has prepared you to receive the abundant rewards.

The Principle of Reciprocity

Understanding Reciprocity

Reciprocity is a natural law that underscores the idea that what you give comes back to you. When you give selflessly, the universe rewards you, though not always in material ways. The payback can manifest as deeper connections, new opportunities, a sense of purpose, and a more fulfilling life. Genuine giving creates a positive energy that attracts goodwill and opens doors to unexpected benefits. This positive energy fosters a cycle of kindness and generosity, encouraging others to follow your example and creating a supportive and enriching environment for everyone involved.

Jim Rohn once said, "The more you give, the more you receive." This quote captures the simple truth that generosity creates abundance. By giving more, you open yourself up to receiving blessings in unexpected ways.

In the last chapter, we talked about how one of the biggest outcomes of becoming a GIVER is the improvement in your relationships. I've noticed that the universe has paid me back through stronger connections with my wife, my boys, my friends and family, and even at work. As these relationship improvements accumulated, I found myself becoming more confident as a GIVER. I was happier.

The universe finds many ways to pay you back for your selfless giving. I'm sure you will discover rewards that aren't even mentioned in this book. Keep an eye out for them—they come in all shapes, sizes, and circumstances.

Manifesting Abundance Through Giving

Mindset of Abundance

To truly embrace the GIVER Method, adopting a mindset of abundance is essential. This mindset shifts focus from scarcity and competition to a belief that there is enough for everyone. By believing in abundance, you trust that your acts of giving will lead to greater returns, even if they are not immediately visible. This perspective allows you to give freely, knowing that the universe will reciprocate in its own time and way. It's about understanding that the more you give, the more you create a flow of enoucraging energy that benefits everyone, including yourself.

Fayette Howard once said, "Kindness is a boomerang. It always returns." Manifesting abundance involves cultivating a mindset and taking actions that allow you to experience more of what you desire in life. This can include:

Material Abundance: Financial security, attracting opportunities that bring wealth, or having enough resources to meet your needs and wants.

Emotional Abundance: Feeling joy, love, gratitude, and fulfillment in your relationships and life experiences.

Physical Abundance: Good health, vitality, and access to resources that support your physical well-being.

Time Abundance: Feeling like you have enough time to do the things that matter most to you.

Experiential Abundance: Having a rich and fulfilling life full of meaningful experiences and personal growth.

Recognizing the Universe's Payback

Practice Gratitude: Keeping a gratitude journal is a powerful way to record moments of giving and the positive feelings associated with them. This practice helps solidify the connection between your acts of generosity and the rewards that follow, fostering a deeper appreciation for the impact of your giving.

There are many ways to weave gratitude into the fabric of your daily life. You might try taking gratitude walks, where you stroll through nature and mentally list everything you're thankful for. The combination of physical activity and mindful appreciation can be incredibly powerful. Or consider creating a gratitude jar: jot down things you're grateful for on small slips of paper and drop them in. On tough days, reading through these notes can remind you of all the good in your life.

Writing gratitude letters is another meaningful practice. Pen heartfelt notes to people who've positively impacted your life, expressing your appreciation for their influence. You don't even need to send these letters; the act of writing them can be beneficial in itself. For a more meditative approach, set aside a few minutes each day to reflect on what you're grateful for. This can be a great way to start or end your day on an upbeat note.

To keep your gratitude practice fresh, try using daily prompts. Ask yourself questions like, "What's something someone did for me recently that I appreciate?" or "What's a challenge I overcame that I'm grateful for?" You might also consider finding a gratitude partner - a friend or family member to share one thing you're each grateful for daily. This not only helps you practice gratitude but also strengthens your relationship.

Visual reminders can be powerful too. Create a gratitude board or collage with images and words representing things you're thankful for. Place it somewhere you'll see it often as a visual reminder of the good in your life. Finally, try incorporating gratitude into your daily routines. For example, before each meal, take a moment to appreciate the food and the people who made it possible.

As part of writing this book, I began keeping a gratitude journal. Initially, I started by listing those who were helping me along the way. Over time, this list grew significantly. At the time of writing this chapter, the list already had 92 people on it. After this chapter, you'll find many of the names of those I am deeply grateful for, as they were willing to help in any way they could. Some may not have known how much they actually helped me, but their contributions were invaluable.

As I made this list, I have been constantly thinking of ways to give back to them. I may never be able to fully repay them for their help, but I am committed to trying. Be sure to take time at the end of this chapter to detail how the universe is paying you back in the short time you have been working on the GIVER Method. Recognizing these moments of gratitude will deepen your appreciation for the journey and inspire you to continue giving selflessly.

Practical Steps to Manifest Abundance

LeRoy Brown said, "You can't go through life collecting moments. You have to create moments and give them away." This highlights that real joy comes from creating special moments and sharing them with others, reminding us that true fulfillment is found in giving.

Manifesting abundance is a journey, not a destination. It involves:

Clarity: Clearly define what abundance means to you in each area of your life. Set specific, achievable goals that reflect your vision of abundance.

Belief: Cultivate a strong belief that you deserve abundance and have the power to create it. Practice daily visualization by spending a few minutes each day imagining your goals and the life you want to create. Use affirmations to reinforce your belief in your ability to attract and create abundance.

Action: Take inspired steps towards your goals and remain open to receiving abundance in unexpected ways. Proactively work towards achieving your goals and be receptive to new opportunities. Maintain a joyous mindset and focus on the possibilities the universe presents.

By integrating these practices into your daily life, you can attract a wealth of positive experiences, relationships, and resources. Embrace abundance, and allow the universe to respond.

Real-Life GIVER Stories

Here are some real-life stories and statements from GIVERs who have embraced their gifts and superpowers without expecting anything in return. These examples illustrate the impact that selfless giving can have on both the giver and the recipients.

Todd T. - *Influencing kids to recognize the superpowers that reside in themselves:*

By dressing up as a real superhero, I embody hope, courage, and inspiration for children. My presence ignites their imaginations and shows them that heroes exist in the real world. I offer them a beacon of light, encouraging them to believe in their own strength and potential. These actions remind them that kindness, bravery, and hope can make a difference.

I was at a one on one charity event a handful of years ago for an 8 year old boy with a terminal illness dressed as Captain America. I remember at one point during the visit he asked me for a fist bump so he could use his superpower which was stealing other heroes' powers to heal himself. I was happy to oblige and I watched his eyes light up. Little did I know that there was some magic in that fist bump. I left the house without thinking much about it, only that I was sad for this young man and his family. Well, here's where the gift was returned. I was getting gas at a local gas station after doing another charity event as Captain America, when an older gentleman approached me. He walked up and asked if he could shake my hand as he recognized me from another event. That other event was the previously mentioned event for the 8 yr old boy. When he began telling me how he knew me I watched his eyes light up and I was kinda confused. Then he shared with me how the young boy has overcome the odds and beat cancer. And how the boy swears to this day it was Captain America's power that saved him....

Aseel E. - *Simplifying complex ideas and distilling power making people feel safe, heard and seen*

People feel supported by me about whatever issue they bring. It allows them to open up about things they never can to someone else, which gives them the power to reflect and grow.

Bridget L. - *Speaking effectively, emotional intelligence, being able to read the room and body language*

I've used my gifts and superpowers to help train empathy at work and improved company satisfaction surveys, improved interpersonal relationships and made the department a more enjoyable experience for all.

Gwen L. - *Creatively solving places where others get stuck*

I helped someone close to me who was stuck on how they should move forward on a book idea. I offered lots of options and ideas and they were able to find one that resonated with them. They gathered my creative ideas and took off with it to move forward on completing their book.

Craig D. - *Dealing with the unexpected*

Dealing with a key employee who had wiped out his finances on cocaine and felt all was lost. I had never dealt with this type of situation and was pretty much put on the spot to help without any advance notice or time to think. I was able to help him separate himself from the "all is lost" emotion and help with a path to financial recovery. Long story short, he continued on as a valued employee for many years.

Scott D. - *A unique balance of "left-brained" and "right-brained" skills*

While most tend to lean one way or the other, I have an unusual balance. I'm able to take large amounts of information and distill it down to a few clear points. Hyper-focus on a task or area of life. Admittedly, this can be a kryptonite when taken too far. I'm also able to ask good questions.

My wife is really good at emotional intelligence, This sometimes puts her in tough situations with another person, her emotions can overwhelm her. That can lead to her to being unsure of how to help or what to say. My ability to listen, ask good questions, and distill down a lot of information helps her take the next step in that situation.

Josh A. - *Empathy- the ability to understand and share the feelings of another*

Empathy is something that I feel I have gained over the course of my life and it is one of the most effective tools that I have as a nurse. There have been several times where I have cared for a patient and later found out that they were related to or knew someone I know. The care I gave usually gets back to that person and then I hear about it from them. It feels great to hear from others that I did a good job with their friend or family member.

Robb G. - *Helping people create the courage to take bold leaps and Finding the engaging storyline/angle to people's messaging*

I've done HUNDREDS of zero expectation connection calls with people. Where my intention is to just show up/help/give. Nothing else. I'm blown away by how frequently those folks end up sending unsolicited referrals my way.

Claudia C. - *Healer - in mind, body and spirit*

As a part of my advocacy work, I am a certified Radical Remission Coach. A prospective client with cancer reached out asking for coaching. She was unable to financially invest in coaching, so I gifted her 5 sessions with me. As a part of those sessions, we uncovered suppressed emotions surrounding her relationship with her daughters. Through the 5 sessions, she reconnected with her daughters and found a deeper connection to her reasons for living. The Universe pay back was in what I received from that experience - confirmation in the work I do and alignment with my purpose.

Majeed M. - *My superpower is to be the bringer of fun*

How did you use your gifts and superpowers: A time I used my superpower is when I formed an impromptu karaoke party at a high end retreat. I was asked to come back to be "the bringer of fun" once a month at all of this company's events, resulting in hundreds of thousands of dollars in referrals for my public speaking coaching business.

Gwen B. - *Compassion*

One instance is when I helped some families who were refugees in this country. We drove to the border and picked them up and helped them resettle in another state near their sponsor. It was a marvelous experience to show compassion to them for all they had been through. The universe's payback came when I received compassion from my friends last year after I was in a serious accident. Within

24 hours of my injury my porch was filled with wheelchairs, walkers, shower chairs and the kitchen was full of food for us. For 2-3 weeks people showered us with assistance and love. I truly believe it is because I share so much with others too. I believe that the hand that gives, gathers! And we don't do this to receive, we do all that we do out of love for others. People have enough grief and burdens to carry. I try to help out as much as I can.

Gayle B. - *A love activator, helping people know they are love and create from that place*

How did you use your gifts and superpowers: I try to find ways that I can help people know they are loved. I look for those opportunities everywhere I go. I was at a festival and I saw a pair of what is called "love specs". I bought them because they are amazing, I wanted to gift them to someone else to help them see love, and because the charity selling them is so good at what they do. I was able to connect well with those from the charity at the festival. It turned out that the charity that had the perfect contact for me to set up the charitable project I had wanted to start for the last 2 years. Because I wanted to use my gift of being a love activator the universe paid me back by helping me connect with this charity and helping me launch the project I was so passionate about. I launched it with the charity. We ended up impacting 100s of families in poverty building a nursery and I became the UK director helping to raise almost 100k and building a beautiful community of fundraisers.

Matt I. - *Music*

I would say my talent in music is my unique gift. I'm not the greatest singer but I CAN sing and it brings me immense joy. I've served as the childrens music leader at church multiple times and, while it can sometimes be stressful, it's a lot of fun.

Every time I'm asked to be the music leader or to sub as the music leader, I hesitate to say yes. It requires me to be a little more extroverted than I'm usually comfortable with. However, I always feel so happy that I did it afterwards and feel that life tends to just go more smoothly. Some might say that is the universe paying back.

Clare K. - *Perception and advocacy*

Seeing and saying, I notice all the things and when I come across something that feels unfair or disrespectful to me or those around me, I am compelled to speak up.

I'm constantly advocating for myself and others. How it's coming back to me but perhaps it's in finally being able to recognize that this advocacy work is at the forefront. I was recently invited to join the global Hidden Disabilities

Sunflower Program as the Regional Director in Canada. It's a part-time commitment and I'm allowed to promote my other work. It is so fully aligned that I think it will unlock incredible opportunities. I've already had a media interview and been invited to a meeting with a senior exec at one of our biggest banks.

Your Call to Action

The journey doesn't end here; it's an ongoing process of learning, growing, and giving. Here are some key steps to keep in mind as you move forward:

Continuous Practice: Regularly apply the principles of the GIVER Method in your interactions. Keep focusing on giving without expecting anything in return, and remain attentive to the needs of others.

Mentoring Others: Share your knowledge and experiences with others. By mentoring and guiding others in the GIVER Method, you can spread its impact even further. Help others discover their gifts and learn how to give selflessly.

Regular Reflection: Make it a habit to reflect on your journey regularly. Use the worksheets and exercises provided to assess your progress, recognize the universe's payback, and celebrate your milestones.

Stay Open to Learning: Always be open to new learning experiences. The more you give, the more you will discover about yourself and the world around you. Embrace every opportunity to learn and grow from your acts of giving.

As Albert Einstein once said, "We can only have real satisfaction if we live for something outside ourselves." Selfless giving is what brings genuine happiness and contentment.

Join the Online GIVER Community

As you continue your journey as a GIVER, we want to stay connected and support your ongoing growth and impact. To further support your journey, we offer a range of additional resources and coaching available at thegivermethod.com. Here, you can become part of the Impact Makers community—a group of GIVERs dedicated to making a bigger impact in the world. Explore our various offerings, including:

- Workshops and Webinars: Participate in interactive sessions that delve deeper into the GIVER Method principles and provide practical strategies for applying them in your life.
- One-on-One Coaching: Receive personalized guidance and support from experienced coaches who can help you navigate your unique challenges and maximize your impact as a GIVER.

- Community Forums: Connect with other GIVERs, share your experiences, and gain valuable insights from a supportive network of like-minded individuals.

- Exclusive Content: Access articles, videos, and other resources that offer advanced tips, success stories, and inspiration to keep you motivated on your GIVER journey.

We invite you to sign up for our email list to receive more insights, stories, and updates on the GIVER Method. By joining our community, you will be among the first to hear about new resources, upcoming events, and opportunities to connect with fellow GIVERs.

To thank you for completing the book, we offer a special downloadable resource or access to an exclusive video series. These materials are designed to deepen your understanding of the GIVER Method and provide practical tips to enhance your giving journey.

Hashtag Use:

To share your story with the broader community, use specific hashtags such as #GIVER, #GIVERMethod, and #IMPACTMakers on social media. These hashtags will help you connect with others who are also practicing the GIVER Method. By sharing your story, you contribute to a larger movement of kindness and generosity.

Take a moment to reflect on your growth with these questions:

- How has understanding and using your unique gifts changed your approach to relationships and interactions?

- In what ways have your acts of selfless giving led to deeper connections and new opportunities?

- How has your perspective on giving and receiving evolved since you began this journey?

- What specific instances stand out where you felt the universe paying you back for your selflessness?

Exercises and Actionable Content

This chapter's actionable content observations on the full journey with reflection prompts, transformation story worksheets, and more.

You can access the Chapter 11 worksheet by going to www.thegivermethod.com/chapter-11-worksheets

Bonus: 30-Day GIVER Challenge Exercise

The 30-Day GIVER Challenge is designed to help you integrate the principles of The GIVER Method into your daily life. This challenge encourages you to actively apply what you've learned over the course of the next month, making selfless giving a consistent part of your routine.

Daily Action Plan:

Each day, document a specific action focused on different aspects of The GIVER Method. These actions can range from small gestures of kindness to more significant acts of generosity. The key is to be intentional about your giving and to focus on a different aspect of the method each day. Whether it's using your unique gifts to help someone, creating value without expecting anything in return, or engaging deeply with someone through active listening and empathy, ensure that your daily actions reflect the core principles of the GIVER Method.

Positive Returns:

As you go through the challenge, make a note of the positive outcomes you observe from your actions. These returns can be tangible, like a smile from a stranger or a thank-you note from a colleague, or intangible, such as a deeper sense of fulfillment or increased self-awareness. Pay attention to how your acts of giving impact both you and those around you. This practice will help you appreciate the reciprocal nature of giving and recognize the ways in which the universe pays you back.

Reflection Notes:

At the end of each day, take a few minutes to write down your reflections on the experience. Consider the following questions as you reflect:

- What did you do today that embodied the GIVER Method?
- How did this action make you feel?
- What positive returns did you notice?
- How did this experience contribute to your personal growth or impact others?

Writing daily reflections will help you track your progress, stay mindful of your journey, and reinforce the positive habits you're developing.

Acknowledgments and Gratitudes

Honoring the Support and Inspiration Behind This Journey

This book is a testament to the GIVER Method and the power of friendship, mentorship, caffeine, and a LOT of editing. Huge thanks to the amazing people who shared their gifts and superpowers with me and who helped turn my word vomit into something coherent. Your selfless contributions have made this journey possible, and I am deeply grateful for each of you.

Some of you know exactly how you helped me on this journey, while others might wonder, "Me? Really? How did I help?" Believe me when I say that each and every one of you has been instrumental in creating the GIVER Method and bringing this book to life. Whether it was through your ideas, help with structure, or editing; your mentorship, coaching, or inspiration; or even a casual conversation or small words of encouragement, your contributions have made a significant impact. Thank you for who you are, how you show up, and for sharing your gifts and superpowers with me.

First and foremost my family Sara, Peter, Cooper, and Sam Skywalker

And to all of you:

Alex Catoni	Brad Martineau	Erin Thomas
Alex Charfen	Bre Gwen	Esther Van Galen
Amanda Carpenter	Brett Cunningham	Gareb Shamus
Amanda Stradling	Bridget Lachance	Gayle Berry
Amiee Ingebrigtsen	Cal Misener	Giovanni Marsico
Andrea Reindl	Charlie Hoehn	Glory Ramsey
Andy Hettrich	Clare Kumar	Greg Jenkins
Archangel Council Members	Claudia Cometa	Hailey Hunter Hines
Archangel Synergy Members	Clint Hosman	Hal Elrod
Amber Sweener	Cole Sundem	Jack Smithson
Aseel El-Baba	Craig de Fassell	Jackie Dumain
Ashlie Vickery	Cyrus Gorjipour	James Tonn
Becky Dresser	Dad	Jason Gaddis
Becky Mackendrick	Davide Viola	Jean-Francois Lacasse
	Dave Kenney	Jeff Spencer
	Dr. Nima Rahmany	Jennifer Kem
	Dr. Stephanie Estima	Jennifer Lyall
	Dyan Abbott	

228

Jennifer Sparkman

Joe Folley

Joe Polish

John Bellamy

John Sparkman

John Stix

Josh Abbott

Joshua B Lee

Joshua Talbert

Justin Eckenroad

Katie Driggs

Katie Witmer

Katrina Fisher

Kevin Thompson

Kiri-Maree Moore

Kiva Schuler

Kyle Brown

Laurie Teal

Lisa Catto

Lou Redmond

Louisa Jewell

Majeed Mogharreban

Mark Jagger

Martha Krejci

Martin Lesperance

Matt Ingebrigtsen

Megan Wright

Mike Krejci

Mom

M Shannon Hernandez

Nate Wright

Neil Moore

Nick Nanton

Paul Decottignies

Peter Katz

Phillipe Brouillard

Rachel Cunningham

Robb Gilbear

Sally Hogshead

Samantha Moonsammy

Samantha Skelley

Sarah Hosman

Scott de Fassell

Sherrie Rose

Simon Bowen

Suze Kenney

Suzy Ashworth

Sachin Patel

Taki Moore

Todd Teal

Tony Kolodziej

Zach Lindquist

I'm sure I've missed a name or two from this list. Despite my efforts to keep a running tally throughout the process, someone will inevitably notice their absence and think, "Hey, I helped, but my name's not here." If that's you, please know that I am deeply grateful for your support, and I apologize for any oversight. Your contribution, no matter how my memory may have faltered, is sincerely appreciated. Thank you for being a part of this journey.

Author's Note

An Open Apology Letter - Owning My Actions and Their Impact

To You,

I know that there will be those who read this book and think, "Yeah, but he's not like that," or, "Your teaching is the opposite of my experience with you," or some other thought contrary to what I am teaching in *The GIVER Method*. I want to take this moment to acknowledge you, my actions, and how they have impacted you.

Over the years, I have struggled with many things like anger, selfishness, depression, anxiety, envy, frustration, guilt, shame, loneliness, jealousy, grief, apprehension, apathy, and hopelessness. Because of these emotions, I know I have done and said things that are hurtful, painful, demeaning, inconsiderate, disrespectful, alienating, destructive, belittling, insensitive, and wounding. These struggles haven't always allowed me to be the best version of myself.

If you are one of the people I have hurt, I am deeply sorry. I know that I will never fully understand the negative impact I may have had on you, your life, and our relationship. I wish I could change that, but what has happened in the past cannot be undone. All I can do is express my regrets and ask for forgiveness.

There comes a day when we all wake up and begin to re-evaluate who we are and who we are impacting. This happened for me, not all at once, but through a series of rude awakenings, reflections, and discussions. I have come to realize that I have been the source of negativity in your life.

I have used these experiences to motivate me to work on myself and become a better person. Through a lot of reflections and personal work, I believe the concepts of The GIVER Method emerged.

It has been a long journey of growth to come to these realizations and to be dedicated to improving myself so I can make a positive impact on your lives. I know I am not perfect, and I will likely do or say something in the future that has a negative impact as well, but know that I am continuing to develop myself into becoming the GIVER and Impact Maker that I want everyone who reads this book to become as well.

I hope this book will serve you as you work to develop and grow yourself. I hope that someday I can be a GIVER to you and share my gifts and superpowers with you to help make any amends possible. Thank you for reading.

With deepest apologies and love,
Jake

About the Author

Jake Talbert is the Founder and Chief GIVER at The GIVER Method and IMPACT Makers, whose journey from struggling employee to thriving business leader embodies the principles he teaches. After feeling trapped in corporate life, Jake discovered he had gifts and superpowers that needed to be shared with the world. Like many, Jake was ready to step into who he was meant to be and use his gifts and superpowers to make an impact in the world.

With over a decade of experience in business coaching and consulting, Jake has guided countless small businesses and individuals to streamline their operations and achieve remarkable growth. As a managing partner at SixthDivision, he helped transform how many small businesses approach their operations, helping entrepreneurs scale while maintaining work-life balance.

Jake's path to creating The GIVER Method was shaped by the many facets of his life. From serving those in his community, where he learned the value of giving without expecting anything in return, to building cosplay armor, where he learned to release his creativity and push past imposter syndrome and have pride in his cosplay builds when taking them to conventions, to his fifteen years in improv comedy, where he learned invaluable lessons about connection, timing, and authentic engagement. These experiences, combined with his business acumen and passion for helping others, led to the development of The GIVER Method—a framework that helps people discover their gifts and use them to create meaningful impact.

Beyond his professional work, Jake serves in various leadership roles within his church community, putting The GIVER Method principles into practice daily. His commitment to service extends beyond business, demonstrating how selfless giving creates positive change in all areas of life.

Jake's greatest joy comes from his family—his wife Sara and their three boys, Peter, Cooper, and Sam Skywalker. They continue to inspire his work and prove that The GIVER Method's principles can transform family dynamics and deepen relationships.

Through The GIVER Method and IMPACT Makers, Jake now shares his insights with others, helping them uncover their unique gifts and superpowers to create meaningful change in their lives and communities. His story stands as living proof that when you discover your gifts and share them generously, you invite the universe to pay you back in remarkable ways.

- The GIVER Method On Facebook: @thegivermethod

- Jake On Facebook: @the.real.jake.talbert

- The GIVER Method Instagram: @thegivermethod

- Jake On Instagram: @the.real.jake.talbert

- YouTube: @thegivermethod

- TikTok: @thegivermthod

- LinkedIn: @TheGIVERMethod

- Website: thegivermethod.com

thank you

Thank You For Reading
The GIVER Method

I love hearing how you're using these ideas to make an impact in your world. Your stories and feedback mean so much to me.

Would you take two minutes to share your thoughts in an Amazon review? Your insights will help make future versions even better and guide others on their GIVER journey.

Keep giving!
Jake

My Gift To You

I am so glad you're here!

As my Gift to you, get FREE Access to the Audiobook of The GIVER Method and other Free Book Bonuses by scanning the QR Code below or visiting TheGiverMethodBook.com